D0195009

RENEWALS 458-4574

DATE DUE

MAY 01			
DEC 13			
MAR 0 4			
APR 2 0 2008			
GAYLORD			PRINTED IN U.S.A.

The Practitioner Inquiry Series

Marilyn Cochran-Smith and Susan L. Lytle, *SERIES EDITORS*

ADVISORY BOARD: Rebecca Barr, Judy Buchanan, Robert Fecho, Susan Florio-Ruane, Sarah Freedman, Karen Gallas, Andrew Gitlin, Dixie Goswami, Peter Grimmett, Gloria Ladson-Billings, Roberta Logan, Sarah Michaels, Susan Noffke, Marsha Pincus, Marty Rutherford, Lynne Strieb, Carol Tateishi, Polly Ulichny, Diane Waff, Ken Zeichner

Teaching Other People's Children

Literacy and Learning in a Bilingual Classroom

WITHDRAWN
UTSA LIBRARIES

CYNTHIA BALLENGER

FOREWORD BY COURTNEY CAZDEN

Teachers College, Columbia University
New York and London

For Jack, and for Emmanuel, Jérémie, Kenthea, Eveline, Giles, Suzanne, and the others.

Published by Teachers College Press, 1234 Amsterdam Avenue, New York, NY 10027

Copyright © 1999 by Teachers College, Columbia University

The following chapters have appeared elsewhere, in an earlier form:

Chapter 4 appeared as "Control in the Classroom: Haitian and American Strategies," in *Harvard Education Review*, Spring 1992.

Chapter 5 appeared as "Learning the ABCs in a Haitian Preschool: A Teacher's Story," in *Language Arts*, 1996, volume 73, number 5.

Parts of Chapters 6 and 7 appeared as "Approaches to Literacy in a Haitian Preschool" in *Teacher Research*, 1996, volume 4, number 1.

All rights reserved. No part of this publication may be reproduced or transmitted in any form or by any means, electronic or mechanical, including photocopy, or any information storage and retrieval system, without permission from the publisher.

Library of Congress Cataloging-in-Publication Data

Ballenger, Cynthia.
    Teaching other people's children: literacy and learning in a bilingual classroom / Cynthia Ballenger; foreword by Courtney Cazden.
       p.   cm. – (The practitioner inquiry series)
    Includes bibliographical references (p.) and index.
    ISBN 0-8077-3789-5 (paper : alk. paper)
    ISBN 0-8077-3790-9 (cloth : alk. paper)
    1. Children of immigrants—Education (Preschool)—United States—Case studies.
2. Haitian Americans—Education (Preschool)—United States—Case studies.   3.
Language arts—(Preschool)—United States—Case studies.   4. Home and school—
United States—Case studies.   5. Education, Bilingual—United States—Case studies.
6. Ballenger, Cynthia.   7. Special education teachers—United States—Biography.
I. Title.   II. Series.
LC3746.B336 1999
370.117'5—dc21   98-47545

ISBN 0-8077-3789-5
ISBN 0-8077-3790-9

Printed on acid-free paper
Manufactured in the United States of America

06 05 04 03 02 01   00 99 8 7 6 5 4 3

Library
University of Texas
at San Antonio

CONTENTS

FOREWORD

During the month in which I first read this remarkable book, I had talked with teachers of Aboriginal children in Alice Springs, Australia, and Native-American children in Juneau, Alaska. Despite the big differences between these indigenous cultures, there are also similarities in the challenges faced by mainstream white teachers trying to do their best by their students. Cindy Ballenger catches perhaps the essence of these similarities early in this autobiographical account of one such teacher. Looking across her particular cultural fault lines, she recounts a conversation with one little boy just returned from living for three years with his godmother in Haiti and then reflects on its meaning, to him and to her:

> I began with these children expecting deficits, not because I believed they or their background were deficient—I was definitely against such a view—but because I did not know how to see their strengths. This is the story of how I came to see their strengths, strengths like Emmanuel's that are part of an intellectual tradition, not always a schooled tradition but an intellectual one nevertheless, and one that, therefore, has a great deal to say to teaching and learning.

Many people have remarked on the challenges confronting teachers who face children each morning from lives far from their own, especially now when that challenge can determine teachers' success across the country. For many years I thought the problem could be alleviated, even if not solved, by providing information about cultural differences as a part of pre-service and in-service education. Recently, Hugh Mehan and I have worried that such information, transmitted in readings and lectures about disembodied "others," may do more harm than good (Cazden & Mehan, 1989). With the best of intentions, it may reinforce, even create, stereotypes and lower expectations, and the information transmitted may make teachers less observant of their students rather than more.

Instead, a more helpful process seems to be for teachers to learn *experientially* about students and families, and in the process to reflect on their own personal and cultural background instead of unthinkingly living it as an unexamined norm. But saying that only changes the terms of the problem; solving it is now up to each teacher. The gift to us in this book is Cindy's straightforward and courageously honest account of such experiential learning—first about classroom control, and then about the heart of her curriculum—storybooks and the ABCs.

That learning happened through Cindy's careful observational records and through her reflections on them in conversations in two discourse worlds outside her classroom. One is the world of the Haitian social service agency of which the preschool center is a part, and the class on Child Development she conducted for Haitian adults who hoped to get jobs in early childhood education. Here Cindy could consult, in Creole whenever necessary, with Haitian parents and colleagues. Admittedly, in this center, space and time as well as people are more easily available for such learning than in many public schools (see, for example, Dyson, 1995). But the catalyst has to be the teacher's awareness of her lack of understanding and her initiative in reaching out for help.

The other world is the teacher-research group of which Cindy is a long-time member. If the role of members of this group were not included, explicitly at the beginning and end of the book and as voices in Cindy's mind throughout, it would be easy to consider this book just the latest in the genre of teacher autobiographies, like the ones that influenced her by Herbert Kohl or Sylvia Ashton-Warner or even Vivian Paley—the story of one individual working in wondrous ways, but working largely alone.

Because of her involvement in these two discourse worlds, Cindy is not working alone. Conversations at the center connect her more closely to her children and beyond them to Haiti. Conversations in the research group connect her to disciplined forms of inquiry, and beyond them to research literature and to researchers themselves. Together, these observations and conversations—"texts" of several kinds, as Cindy explains—add up to a far more powerful example of "professional development" than many activities dignified and justified by that easy name.

—*Courtney Cazden*

REFERENCES

Cazden, C.B. & Mehan, H. (1989). Principles from sociology and anthropology: Context, code, classroom and culture. In M. Reynolds (Ed.), *Knowledge base for the beginning teacher* (pp. 47–57). Oxford and New York: Pergamon.

Dyson, A.H. (1995). "What difference does difference make? Teacher perspectives on diversity, literacy, and the urban primary school." *English Education, 27,* 77–139.

Acknowledgments

My research into my teaching and my students began in 1989 when I joined the Brookline Teacher Seminar. All the members have played a role in my thinking: Susan Black, Cindy Beseler, Ericka Herndon, Karen Gallas, Steve Griffin, Betsy Kellogg, Sarah Michaels, Catherine O'Connor, Mary Oldenburg, Jim Swaim, Roxanne Pappenheimer, and Ann Phillips. Without them, this wouldn't have been half as much fun or as interesting.

Jim Gee and Catherine O'Connor were my dissertation advisors. It was Jim's idea that I could write about my classroom as my dissertation. Until he suggested this, I had no idea that my classroom research and my academic research might meet. Cathy then helped shape my dissertation so that it could indeed be rigorous and honest, and still live in both worlds.

Many Haitian friends and colleagues helped me understand my students, but above all Josiane Hudicourt-Barnes, whose friendship and intellectual support for my work pushed my own energy and commitment.

My colleagues at the Chèche Konnen Center have also been crucial sources of support—reading drafts, understanding absences, valuing the endeavor—especially Mary Bodwell, Ann Rosebery, and Beth Warren.

My son Michael read chapters and engaged with me in many conversations, bringing his own unique perspective on education. My daughter Catherine volunteered at the school, became a friend to my young students, and shared some of my own difficulties crossing cultures. My husband, Jack, knows his contributions are beyond description.

I was fortunate to receive some small grants that helped me to write. The National Council of Teachers of English gave me a teacher-researcher grant that helped to support the work on the ABCs. I received a Mellon Research Training Grant from the Literacies Institute in Newton, Massachusetts, that helped in the preparation of the chapter on control talk. The Spencer Foundation has given support to the Brookline Teacher Researcher Seminar, of which I am a member. I am deeply grateful to each of these organizations.

Chapter 1

INTRODUCTION

Emmanuel entered my classroom at St. George's school one winter day when he was almost 4 years old. Formally dressed in slacks and loafers, he was presented for school by his mother. He had just returned from Haiti, where his mother had been born and grown up. Emmanuel was born in the United States, but when his mother lost her babysitter, when he was less than 2 years old, she sent him back to Haiti to live with a close family friend, his godmother. Emmanuel's mother and his older brother, who was in first grade, remained here. When he was was old enough for day care and a slot for him could be found, Emmanuel returned. He had been gone for almost 2 years. He arrived in my classroom speaking only Haitian Creole, eager for friendship but also subject to long and intense bouts of angry crying. As we became acquainted, he told me in bits and pieces about his experience in Haiti: about his godfather, who was hospitalized with a broken leg, the garden they planted; about the plane trip to Haiti and the cassette tapes his mother sent periodically, which substituted for phone calls, and by which, eventually, his return was arranged.

He was, it became clear, a lively and intelligent little boy, but it concerned me that I would often find him alone talking about his trip to Haiti and his return. He would sit by himself, sometimes facing the wall, and talk in what seemed to me to be a disconnected fashion, a sort of bare chronology of the events: "I went to Haiti in an airplane. I came back to my house." It also concerned me that he would sometimes attach himself to women he did not know well, another child's mother or a grandmother from the kitchen staff. This kind of separation was not an uncommon event among the Haitian families I knew—parents and children often had to be separated for economic reasons. I was not surprised to see Emmanuel's difficulties but I worried about them all the same.

One day Emmanuel arrived at school and came directly to find me. He announced: "You know, Cindy, I didn't always live with Joel [his brother]/ M pa t toujou rète avèk Joel." I responded, "You didn't?/se vre?" He continued:

Ou konnen m pa toujou nan mèm kote lè m te piti
Maman m voye m al Ayiti.
Li voye bibon mwen

Li voye beso mwen
Pou me ka bwe
Pou ma ka dòmi
Lakay nennenn m.

You know I was not in this same place when I was little
My mother sent me to Haiti
She sent my bottle
She sent my crib
So I could drink
So I could sleep
At my godmother's house.   (Emmanuel, 4 years 2 months)

I was struck by this story. I immediately wrote it down. Since Emmanuel knew that I knew he had been in Haiti, I wondered why he announced his story to me in the way he did. And I noticed that he spoke with an unusual confidence. The rhythm of Emmanuel's speech struck me as well—it was cadenced and each phrase was followed by a pause, and then the last phrase "at my godmother's house" was said with a sort of staccatto finality.

I see this as a poem. I've been thinking about this little poem off and on ever since. It was very different from the way he had been talking about this occurrence in his life before. It occurred to me that his mother probably didn't send down his bed—his bottle, yes, but probably not his bed. He was making that part up. As I wondered why, it seemed to me that the bed and the bottle were symbols to him of his mother's continuing care, of her concern that he drink and sleep, of her role as his mother. It didn't matter to Emmanuel whether the bed had actually gone down to Haiti with him. This was not necessarily about what actually happened. He was constructing a narrative that brought meaning—the meaning of his mother's care—to these events.

Emmanuel had struggled to construct the understanding that his poem contained, the understanding that his mother had sent with him her nurturance the best way she could. He had crafted a resonant and symbolic account. He was a young boy, barely 4 years old. He couldn't read or write, knew no letters. In fact he did not know what letters were and was astonished when he realized I could write down speech: "What are you doing? /ki sa ou ap fè?" he had exclaimed one day as I wrote a caption for a picture he had drawn. But he had worked with language in a sophisticated way to bring meaning to what had happened to him. How had he done so?

It seemed to me that this represented a breakthrough for Emmanuel in coming to an understanding of his mother's role in his life. The signs of her care went with him and were taken up by another person at her request.

She did not have to be there to be a mother to him. There are many Haitian proverbs that seem to speak to this situation. One that I misunderstood the first time I heard it goes as follows: "If you can't go to war yourself, send the plume of your hat." I assumed this was an ironic statement about an armchair general—what good could the plume of your hat do if others were truly risking their lives? However, I have been assured by a number of Haitians that the more usual interpretation for this proverb is that you do what you can. The plume of your hat is a fine addition to the effort if that's what you can manage; it conveys your support. Similarly, the bottle and the bed carried Emmanuel's mother support and nurturance.

Many other Haitian proverbs discuss the ability to make do, for example, "When you don't have your mother, nurse from your grandmother," or "The hawk flies, if it cannot find chicken, it takes straw." Emmanuel, I believe, had reached into the resources his culture provided him to make sense of his time away. He had shown me a way of coming to terms with these events that I would not have known, one deeply supported by his background.

The process of appreciating the thought and the imagination that Emmanuel's story contained was not a quick one. I began with these children expecting deficits, not because I believed they or their background were deficient—I was definitely against such a view—but because I did not know how to see their strengths. This is the story of how I came to see their strengths, strengths like Emmanuel's that are part of an intellectual tradition, not always a schooled tradition but an intellectual one nonetheless, and one that, therefore, has a great deal to say to teaching and learning.

THE CHILDREN

St. George's, the school Emmanuel attended, was a preschool run by the Catholic Church in a neighborhood to which a large number of Haitian immigrants had recently come. There were nine children who were in my classroom consistently. Others entered on occasion; the situation was somewhat fluid.

Jean and Jean-Marc were just 4 years old. They were twin boys, always dressed identically. I couldn't tell them apart, although some could. They had big brothers and uncles living with them who spoke English and so English was their preferred language. Their connection to each other was very close; it was unlikely for one to come to school if the other was sick. The one time one of them did come to school without the other, he missed his brother all day. They expected everything to be the same for both of them. One day we read a book that had a dog as the main character; the dog was named Jean. Jean-Marc cried every time that book was brought out—it seemed that it made him feel terrible that there was no dog named Jean-Marc too.

Tatie was the youngest child, a child we enrolled before she was 3 in order to help out her mother. She was absolutely silent in general, but watchful. She rarely joined any activity. Rather, she gave the impression of proceeding quite competently on her own concerns. We would occasionally find that she was following the curriculum, but in her own way—like the time she took and hid all the *T*s in the classroom, magnetic letters, coloring papers, *T*s from the ABC lotto, because she had realized that *T* was for Tatie.

Jérémie attended the school for 3 years. By the time he was in my class he was returning from public school kindergarten in the afternoons. He was a very active boy, beloved by his classmates, often disorganized and messy. He was passionate about stories—he had to hear them. He was the kind of boy who often presents trouble to his teachers, and he did to me—as you will read in Chapter 4, I called his father in at one point to help me. And yet, listening to him on the audiotapes I made in the classroom, I would realize how hard he was working on our joint tasks. As a first grader in public school, he was referred to Special Education, but I think you will see his intelligence at work, particularly in the chapter about storybook reading.

Rubenson's twin sister was in a different class at the school. Their father had only recently managed to bring the children over from Haiti. They were 4 years old and direct from the Haitian countryside. Their father had remarried here, although he was nevertheless in the process of bringing the children's mother to the United States to join them. The Haitian teachers felt that these children had been left to grow up unsocialized in Haiti as evidenced, for example, by the way they looked directly at you as you disciplined them; Haitian children are supposed to look down. I, of course, was quite comfortable with this behavior since American teachers expect children to look right at them in these circumstances.

Kenthea was the calm center of our classroom. She was a solid 5-year-old, peaceful and relaxed. When she was absent, the whole group felt slightly off. Every child was a little more comfortable playing across from her or leaning against her.

Eveline was a 4-year-old girl with beautiful beaded hair, at times hiding her eyes and smiling face. She could balance on one foot on a chair, leap from any height, and land safely. She didn't limit her feats of skill to appropriate times, however, performing them joyfully even on the school bus. I worried about asking her strict parents to help me control her behavior, but, as it happened, a phone call to them quickly brought her behavior within safe limits and didn't diminish her joy at all.

Giles was a tall, slender 5-year-old with beautiful loose curls falling across his face. He was abstracted, a deep thinker, often stumbling over things as he made his way. He loved books and letters and drawing, and his parents and other children.

Emmanuel, the boy with whom I began, never stopped talking. He often seemed to be acting out things he had seen in Haiti, marching around the playground, for example, calling out in a repeated sing-song, "I have no money, looking for fish/pa gen kòb, ap chache pwason." His play always included a song or a chant that expressed what he was doing. The other children would tease him because he, a boy, liked to play "mother." He played near the others but his imagination seemed to be so powerful, leading him here and there at its will, that he could not join in their more negotiated dramas.

Suzanne's mother worked in the nearby church and her aunt was often around the school; she would run to them when she felt unhappy. They both spoke French as well as Creole and were eager for Suzanne to speak French also. She was intelligent and watchful, always negotiating relationships, seemingly never satisfied with them as they were.

Pierre was one of those 4-going-on-40 children. He would ask his special friends, "Wanta go to college with me and become a psychologist?" I don't know what that meant to him. One day my car broke down and my luck was such that his father was driving right behind me. He pulled over when he saw my trouble, and it turned out that he was a mechanic. He fixed my car. When I told this story to some other teachers on my arrival at school, Pierre listened from the periphery; as I finished and everyone laughed at my good luck in encountering his father on the road, Pierre entered the circle of adults and corrected me forcefully in English, "He's not a mechanic. He's a Haitian." He made a point of telling me what he thought I needed to know.

Leslie was another 3-year-old but she was enormously self-possessed. Her father was Cuban and her mother Haitian and she knew all about both countries. Like Pierre she had older sisters, and from their conversations she had figured out a path for her life.

THE TEACHER

The children called me Cindy or Miss Cindy. I was an experienced preschool teacher with a background in Early Childhood Special Education. My classrooms had usually been filled with children with language delays and learning disabilities. Over the years I had noticed, however, that, although I lived in a diverse city, my students were almost entirely poor. Why did so many poor children have trouble with language learning? I had returned to graduate school in Applied Linguistics to understand this. After 3 years in graduate school, having spent some time studying linguistic issues in education, I missed children so desperately that I returned to teaching.

When I met Emmanuel, I had the good fortune to be the only American teacher at St. George's. Emmanuel, the other children, and all the other teachers were Haitian, and both Haitian Creole and English were used in the classroom. Although I speak reasonably good Haitian Creole, I am not an insider to Haitian culture. I was frequently in situations where, although my words were understood, my full intentions were not, whichever language I chose to use. Similarly, I did not always fully understand the intentions and assumptions of the adults and children around me. As the only non-Haitian teacher working in this preschool I was in a situation where what I considered "natural" or "correct" ways to teach small children were evidently not received as such by the children; nor did I understand or appreciate their ways. I could not make my classroom function, nor learning take place, in the way that—after 15 years of experience as a preschool teacher—I expected.

THE BOOK

The title of this book reflects my reading of an important article written by Lisa Delpit (1988), in which she critiques aspects of progressive pedagogy. She suggests that some rules about how to talk and how to act in school are left implicit by teachers like myself, teachers intending to celebrate the differences that children bring to the classroom. Delpit claims that those children who do not learn these particular conventions at home have difficulty acquiring them at school. In many ways this book is an exploration, and I hope a further formulation, of the tension Delpit so importantly identifies—the tension between honoring the child's home discourse as a rich source of knowledge and learning itself, and yet wishing to put that discourse into meaningful contact with school-based and discipline-based ways of talking, acting, and knowing.

In this book I will describe one particular class of Haitian preschoolers and their attempts to engage with me on various aspects of language and literacy; they helped me to see the assumptions I brought to our work together as well as those that they did. This is a book about what counts as knowledge in the classroom and my own attempts to evaluate this in light of daily encounters with these spirited and hard-thinking children.

In Chapter 2 I will describe the traditions and practices of teacher research as I have experienced them, traditions and practices that allowed me to bring my knowledge of culture and language and my experience with children together. In Chapter 3 I will describe the school, the families, and the patterns of family life that I learned about as I taught at St. George's.

The next four chapters are accounts of the difficulties I had in teaching literacy and in behavior management and what I learned from these difficulties. Chapter 4 is an account of the differences I discovered between my assumptions about how adults should control or influence children's behavior and the assumptions of my children and their families. Chapter 5 is an account of early literacy activities, especially learning to write letters, and the different ways my students and I approached these activities. Chapters 6 and 7 are about storybook reading and the ways my students participated imaginatively with storybooks.

In Chapter 6 I explore the ways in which the children distinguished, or failed to distinguish, books and catalogs. I then explore a transcript of their talk as I was reading a book to them. In their talk and participation they appear to be acting out the characters and, at times, changing the story in line with their own interests. Chapter 7 follows another discussion of a book, this time one in which the children wandered far afield and discussed a variety of issues important to them, but not part of the text. In both cases I am interested in how they thought one should behave around a book, and in how they made sense of the book's story in relation to their own lives.

In the final chapter I return to teacher research to consider again some of its important values and how the insights it offers are different from other forms of educational research.

NOTE

1. All names in this book are pseudonyms. Some identifying characteristics have been changed as well.

Chapter 2

TRADITIONS

This is a book made up of stories from the classroom, a very particular classroom where the children I taught and their families had many experiences with which I was unfamiliar, many beliefs about education that differed from mine, and many assumptions about the role of authority, the relationships among children, and ways of playing and learning of which I was not initially aware. It is about how I uncovered and explored the value and meaning of these different ways, as I tried to introduce new or additonal ways as well.

In uncovering and exploring these different practices and beliefs, I became a researcher of my own classroom. I was fortunate to become involved, just as I started teaching at St. George's, with a group of teachers and researchers who wanted to explore what teacher research might mean to us. This group became the Brookline Teacher-Researcher Seminar (BTRS). This is a group of from 8 to 12 teachers who have met once a week after school for the past 8 years to look at transcripts of classroom conversation. We have explored our teaching together, read and written articles together, attended and participated in conferences, collaborated in many ways. In the end I have only my own understanding of the experiences I am about to convey, but I hope to make clear that this road was in no way one that I traveled alone.

While the BTRS was in many ways breaking new ground, both theoretically and practically, for ourselves as we developed our idea of teacher research, we also brought with us traditions from our training and from our reading of accounts of other classrooms. In this chapter I wish to describe the intellectual traditions with which the BTRS began, and then the approaches to education we found useful and enriching as we developed our version of teacher research. I want to do this especially because it seems to me that as teacher research is more and more being seen as a panacea for the problems in our educational sytem, there is little attention paid to the various intellectual foundations and commitments of this work. This book tries to present both examples and explanation of the marriage of theory and practice that I have known in the BTRS.

In my opinion, teacher research is not something that needs to be unified in specific beliefs or methods (Cochran-Smith & Lytle, 1993). Teachers may wish to do research in different ways, drawing on different interpretive frameworks, different methodologies, and different viewpoints on learning. Many approaches may be useful. There is nevertheless advocacy in my description of this form of teacher research. I do believe that what I will describe here, situated as it is in my own experience, is a highly effective model for reflection, for teaching and learning with children, and that it represents a form of teacher research that would be of great value to many different teachers with many different concerns.

As I describe this approach, I want to focus in particular on the values it offers to teaching and to research for diverse classrooms, classrooms such as my own where we did not all share the same cultural background. Let me say before beginning, however, that I have taught in other classrooms, with other children, many of whom did share my background, and I do not think that teaching childen from a culture not your own is ultimately different from teaching children you believe you understand more easily. The differences are less important than the similarities. From the vantage point of teacher research, as I understand it now, teaching children that you *know* you don't always undertand is an advantage—the problem comes when you think you understand. For a teacher-researcher, what is important with all children is to find the challenge to your understanding. Teacher research, as I know it, is letting the children, whoever they are, teach you—both about themselves and about their view of the domain you are jointly studying—while you are teaching them. It is this dual process that I will be attempting to describe here.

THE LEGACY OF THE 1960s

I want to begin by considering aspects of the intellectual history of my own participation in education and educational theorizing, and that of some of my colleagues. This will place teacher research as I know it in the context of the values and the views of schooling and culture that shaped it.

I speak now as one of the members of the BTRS in her forties, as someone who prepared for teaching in the atmosphere of the 1960s and early 1970s. The group includes younger teachers, whose experiences and points of view are influential, particularly now, but the BTRS was in many ways formed by the literature and the attitudes toward education that were a part of that era. In the spirit of that time we entered teaching to help children less fortunate than ourselves, and we entered the profession with a distrust for the norms and conventions of the traditional classroom. We did not trust that the children who were doing badly were truly not intelligent, nor were we convinced that children who did well in school were learning material that was either useful or profound.

We felt very much in tune with the accounts of schooling and teaching current at that time. There were theorists like A. S. Neill, Paul Goodman, and Neil Postman, but for many of us, it was above all teacher-authors such as Sylvia Ashton-Warner, Herbert Kohl, George Dennison, John Holt, and Jonathan Kozol who shaped our view of the problems of classrooms. For many of us, these authors, who spoke with a teacher's voice, were the first to show us how to see the culture children came with and how to begin to see the culture of schooling as well.

For example, Sylvia Ashton-Warner—both in her extended essay *Teacher* (1963) and in her wonderful novel *Spinster* (1958)—gives the reader a sense of her students' Maori culture and of the many ways in which she reflected on it: in relation to her reading program; in relation to the arts, to behavior expectations, and management issues; and in comparison to her own culture. She deplored at times the "overdisciplined European" child, the product of what she calls "respectable parents." She explores the effects of what might be called "proper upbringing" on the imagination and on a dramatic sense of life. An encounter with her work helped us to see that neither background was more "natural" and that each was fully relevant to academic concerns.

Herb Kohl in *36 Children* (1967), like Jonathan Kozol in *Death at an Early Age* (1967), showed us children identified as unteachable, as slow and unreachable, nevertheless demonstrating motivation and intelligence in the unusual classrooms these authors ran. Kohl tells us:

> I read the class novels, stories, poems, brought my library to class and let them know that many people have suffered throughout history and that some were articulate enough to create literature from their lives. . . . We spoke and read about love and madness, families, war, the birth and death of individuals and societies; and then they asked me permission to write themselves. Permission.

Kozol told comparable stories of his students engagement with poetry, poetry that was considered above their level. A common and resonant thread in these works is a view of the arts, of high culture, as a universal ground on which all children can function, a view of stories and poems and drawings and music as something to which all children have access. Their accounts absolutely challenge any reliance on conventional measures of ability or even on past performance to tell us what children are capable of; in fact, these works make the claim that all children can learn.

And yet, at its best, this literature does not offer solutions. It is preeminently the messy voice of practice. Listen to Vivien Paley (1979). Paley had grown up in the South. She was teaching in Chicago when she received her first black child. The child ignored her and appeared afraid, although she got along with the other children. Paley had grown up believing that the way to show respect for black people was never to acknowledge out loud that they were black: "We showed respect by completely ignoring black people as black people" (p. 9), not an unusual mainstream strategy in the 1950s and 1960s. When the children made remarks, hostile and friendly, about color, Paley was unable to respond. One day the black child got hurt—she knocked down another child's block tower and he jumped up and pushed her into the door, yelling "You bad brown doody." The child was bleeding and terribly frightened. Paley felt the child's fear and pain:

> The words rushed out of me. "Alma baby, my pretty colored baby. Now hush y'all. Hush, Alma honey." I heard my voice; it had a sing-song tone that sounded like the Negro women I used to hear from my window in New Orleans. (p. 4)

It is painful to read this example. Was this proper, a white teacher talking in a black way? It was a decision made on the basis of a sense of the time and the place and a relationship, a heavily contextualized decision. But can such situation-specific expertise offer another educator, another individual concerned about language and culture in the classroom, anything of value?

I would argue that the effect of this kind of writing is the effect of a novel: a broadening of experience, the development of intuitions, perhaps the challenging of intuitions or assumptions. The novel's wisdom, according to Milan Kundera in his book *The Art of the Novel* (1988), is "the wisdom of uncertainty"; it is "grounded in the relativity and ambiguity of things human" (p. 13). That the teacher might need to speak in the child's dialect now becomes a possibility to consider, another human response. The detailed attention to these ruptures in the expected pattern of classroom life, and the deeply contextualized presentation of them and of responses to them, is very powerful in this literature. These accounts become in effect another experience that the reader has had and that he or she brings to bear on an always-emerging theory of teaching and learning.

These books, with others, were a part of an opening up of culture and convention, our own as well as others', to critique and reflection. While making many claims about what children could do, they also contained a sense, like a novel, that life in the classroom couldn't be regulated solely by reason and technique, by a priori best practices.

This literature generally took the attitude that children will learn unless impeded from learning. It contained at its core an earlier phrasing of the question that motivates many of the most powerful pieces of teacher research today: Why aren't all children learning? This question was perhaps at first only a rhetorical question among us, one demanding action, expressing concern. It has remained this, but, as we began doing teacher research ourselves, it has become as well another kind of question, one that we can investigate, gather data on, formulate in different ways, a question without final answers perhaps, but one that is behind a union of theory and practice.

To explore the changes in this question, and the movement in the BTRS to the next tradition from which we draw support, we need to go on to Steve's question.

STEVE'S QUESTION

Steve Griffin was a speech and language therapist, and he taught in a highly respected school system adjacent to a major city. The school system where Steve taught participated in a voluntary program of desegregation by which a certain number of inner-city children were able to attend school there. Steve found that a disproportionate number of these children were referred to him for speech and language problems. This was a puzzle and one he wasn't sure how to address at first.

His resolve to find a way to address this puzzle was strengthened when a poet became a part of the schools where he was working. She worked in many classrooms and many of the children became engaged in writing poetry. Steve was surprised to discover that in his case load of children identified as having speech and language difficulties, he had many of the best student poets—these same inner-city youngsters. Steve found himself asking why, if these students had an awareness of language that allowed them to write poetry, they were not performing well in other language-related activities. Were there any other skills that these students had that weren't generally recognized by the school? Were teachers somehow seeing deficits where there were strengths (see Griffin, 1992, 1997)?

Steve began to look for help with his question.[1] He founded the BTRS in collaboration with three linguists interested in language and schooling and a large group of elementary school teachers who had similar questions. This group, which has come to include 10 to 12 teachers and two linguists, has met weekly during the school year since 1989. It formed our introduction to the second intellectual tradition that plays a role in teacher research in this group. This tradition comes from the work of anthropologists such as Dell Hymes and Shirley Brice Heath; educational theorists such as Courtney Cazden and Douglas Barnes; and linguists such as James Gee, Sarah Michaels, and Catherine O'Connor. It is focused on the variety in our ways of using language—and on the effects of this variety.

Among the works we read was an article by Sarah Michaels (1985). Her work focused on carefully analyzed transcripts of the stories children told. In these transcripts we could see that the stories of some students—in general white students—were being shaped and elaborated by the teacher's response; the teacher was working with them collaboratively to develop the detail and structure needed to explain their ideas clearly to others. Other students—the African-American students in particular—were interrupted more often; their stories were deemed too long, confusing, and sometimes untrue. The teacher hadn't seen the point of these stories and hadn't been able to help develop them.

Yet, a careful look through the transcripts revealed richness in the stories of the black students (Gee, 1990; Michaels, 1985). These students were speaking in a style unfamiliar to the teacher. Their stories often contained multiple episodes, which seemed confusing and unorganized but which in fact were often connected thematically and led to a deeper view of the concern the child was working with. Their stories might contain fantastic elements, which were sometimes interpreted as lies, but fantastic elements are a part of a strong and rooted storytelling tradition for many African-American familes. There was attention to repetition and rhythm and sound, which was a part of the literary quality of these stories but was often lost on teachers who were tuned in to explicit language and clear exposition. Because these ways of using language were unexpected, many teachers failed to appreciate them and to see the skill with which the children were employing them. We identified with these teachers. We now had the unsettling sense that we too might be failing to understand some of the students we were particularly trying to help. We saw that what we regarded as incompetent performance in the moment might in fact be highly competent if we had the time to look at it further.

Steve was the first to venture to pursue this vision in his own classroom. He taped himself talking about a math problem with a student whom he found to be difficult. He says that being aware of the tape made him less quick to interrupt the student, who went on explaining herself, heading in what Steve initially thought was a wrong direction. Reading the transcript with the group at a later time, Steve saw sense in her thinking that he had not seen before.

Teacher research in the BTRS began with the tape recorder as a way to "stop time" (Phillips, 1992) in the classroom so that we could listen longer. It began with the literature of sociolinguistics, which gave us stories and actual transcripts in which students were misunderstood by their well-meaning teachers, in which there was more to hear and to understand than first appeared. The practices and insights of sociolinguistics offered us a way to study ourselves and our students as both talkers and listeners.

We had known there were cultural differences, and differences among individuals as well, in ways of talking, and that these were misunderstood and even stigmatized in school—these were views from the 1960s that we were committed to. However, these differences tended to look like deficits to us, no matter what we did. If children hadn't been read storybooks at home, we didn't blame them for their lack of experience. But we still thought of them as behind. We had no way to explore what skills with language and what experiences with stories, for example, they were bringing to school. We had no way to see our own ways of using language, to mine the things that children say for the sense and meaning that was there, to explore the connections between the everyday ways we all talk and academic learning.

We do not take from this work the idea that a child's cultural background determines his or her approach. Rather, I think because we focus on the meaning a child is making, we see our students as more powerful, freer, and more imaginative than we did before. Looking at transcripts has given us new categories, and more expanded categories, through which to look at what might be relevant to schooling, and new ways to make sense of children's behavior and to connect with it. Looking at transcripts, we discover individuals, who constantly break out of categories. Through this approach to data and to interpretation, we have found a way to see what children are putting their energy into, the ways in which they are approaching knowledge of the world, where their skills lie; at the same time, it gives us a way to explore the patterns and assumptions that formed the structure and content of our own teaching.

CONCLUSION

The question that began as "Why aren't all children learning" has changed with our exploration into children's talk. We have been surprised to discover how much many of our seemingly less able students know, how hard they think, how deeply they consider aspects of the curriculum we have long since stopped wondering about. This increased respect for all children doesn't lead us to give up our role as teachers. Although the students are thinking hard and well, they still have more to learn. Our question now is "What is it that they know, and what is it that we know?" I hope that in the following chapters this new question will deepen in the context of examples from my classroom and my students.

NOTE

1. Ann Phillips was of particular help in re-creating this history. See Phillips (1992, 1996) for fuller accounts.

Chapter 3

THE SETTING

In this chapter I will describe St. George's school itself and the patterns of family life that I encountered working there with Haitian families. I have known many Haitian people, all highly individual in various ways, but also people with some beliefs and traditions in common. I will try to describe in this chapter some of the values and traditions that people I know follow in raising their children. In some cases I will return to these concerns in later chapters.

Before beginning, let me say that what I know about Haitian culture comes mainly from discussion with Haitian friends, from questions I've asked them that came out of my experience. While I cite work on Haitian culture in support of my statements about it, they were never the source of my understanding. I don't know how different my understanding would have been if I had studied Haitian culture directly before I began teaching these children. Nevertheless, it is accurate to say that I went into this class-room without any academic knowledge of the particular culture. It seems important to make this point because, with all the endless things that teachers are supposed to be expert on, it is not within my experience to say that they need to be expert on the specific cultural background, narrative style, and literacy experience of each child in the class.

Rather, what is needed—and what helped me—are the attitudes that I had found growing up in the 1960s toward cultural differences: They were a pleasure, a surprise, a source of enrichment. It was an enormous privilege to be included in something beyond your own background. In addition, I was reading and had read a large number of works on cultural and linguistic issues in classrooms. These works, such as *Ways with Words* by Shirley Brice Heath (1983), explored cultural issues relating to African-American culture, to Hawaiian culture, to Navajo culture, and to other cultures. They gave a flexibility to my thinking, a sense of how these differences were a part of a value system and a way of being in the world. They allowed me to recognize my own "culture" in things that I had assumed were natural. I found these works enormously helpful, but they did not explore Haitian culture in particular and I'm not sure that they needed to.

BEGINNINGS

My interest in Haitian culture, my need to know about it, actually preceded my tenure as a teacher at the little school that Emmanuel and the others attended. I was an early childhood special education teacher in a diverse urban community for many years. Over time, as the population of the city changed, I began receiving more and more Haitian children in my class, and they always arrived attended by great concern. A number were referred to me because they had "no language"; others because they were "wild" and their mothers were depressed; a few were also considered retarded. What was odd about all this was that I began "curing" these children. I am not someone who sets a great deal of stock in IQ scores, but I was struck when one boy entered with an IQ score of 70, and left, less than a year later, with an IQ of 107. Those with no language began to speak. The "wild" ones I usually didn't manage to "tame," but they nevertheless began to show their intelligence. And after a time, the depressed mothers would smile.

What was going on? Clearly I was not curing children who had significant disabilities. There was something wrong with our diagnosis. These children were by and large fine. I set out to learn the language and to find out about the culture. I returned to graduate school in applied linguistics. Three years later, now speaking Haitian Creole (HC) reasonably well, I found myself the teacher-director at St. George's and a member of the BTRS.

THE SCHOOL

St. George's was a small private preschool and day care center operated as part of a neighborhood social service agency that served a primarily Haitian clientele. The agency was funded through state and federal money, with some support from Catholic Charities. The school itself was primarily supported by state money, which subsidized the tuition for children whose families met the definition of working poor, and from the tuition paid by families who could afford to pay. However, this began to change as the state attempted to balance its budget by cutting spending in social programs. When I started teaching at the school in September 1988 there were 25 children, out of a total of 30, whose tuition was subsidized in one form or another. Within 2 years the subsidized slots had decreased to five. Since the families that the agency was committed to serving could not afford the tuition without subsidy, we were forced to subsidize their costs out of our operating budget. During these 3 years, the school became more and more hard-pressed. The agency director did the janitorial work. We were short of supplies. We were unable to afford to pay teacher's aides. The food service that provided the children's lunches was not being paid regularly and, consequently, on occasion did not deliver. When I left the school in June 1991 it was largely because I did not have the stamina to continue in a situation of such stress.

And yet, while I identify the situation as stressful, there was simultaneously great camaraderie and cooperation among the staff. The school was jointly run by the teachers. We spent considerable time together each day. In fact, the work that I will report on would not have been possible without the opportunity for talk that this afforded us. It seems important to note that in this way my situation was luxurious compared with that of many public school teachers, who rarely have time to discuss their teaching with colleagues. Schools that also function as day care centers create situations where children really live with you. As our students napped, my friend and colleague, Colette, and I would sit together, and she would tell me stories—sometimes in English, sometimes in Creole—of growing up in Haiti. The children would sleep, or so it would seem until she stopped for some reason. Then one or another little head would pop up, turtle-like, and ask a question or request that she continue. Many of the children had come from Haiti as babies, or had been born in the United States. Some went back regularly, but many did not. They loved to hear her stories.

This was very much a Haitian center. The school buildings shared the grounds with one of the main Haitian Catholic churches in the city. English classes, literacy classes in Haitian Creole, GED classes, immigration counseling, and help with jobs, housing, prenatal care, and AIDS education were among the services the agency provided to the Haitian community. When the roof leaked, when a window was broken, when fuel oil was needed, it was Haitian tradesmen who were called. The school was in the midst of this active community. The Haitian priests were in and out of the school, as were the instructors and clients in these various other programs. As people passed by, they would often stop to chat with the children; in this way I would often find out, for example, that the immigration counselor was the godfather of one of the children, or that a new English teacher was a child's cousin or neighbor. There were so many connections that it frequently seemed to me (it still seems to me) that all Haitians must be related in one way or another.

The children were from 3 to 6—most spent a full day at the school, some came after a half-day of kindergarten to spend the afternoon with us. There were four classrooms, each containing a mix of ages. The children spoke Haitian Creole and English, although they differed in which language they preferred. Most were stronger in Haitian Creole and used it with their friends and frequently with me, and occasionally asked for translations from English into HC. There were a few who, generally because they had older siblings in school, were more accustomed to speaking English. Occasionally French-speaking children would find their way to us: One was a West African child; another was a boy from Cape Verde who was bilingual in Portuguese and French. The teachers all spoke English and Haitian Creole, and used both interchangeably with the children and with each other. We also spoke French with varying degrees of facility, but used it rarely.

The children's parents came from all levels of Haitian society. Most had come to the United States for economic reasons, but political motivations were present as well. In U.S. society, their positions varied as well. Many of the children's mothers worked in nursing homes; the people who arrived with less education were often housekeeping staff while those with more education might be nurse's aides, and a few of the children's mothers were licensed practical nurses or registered nurses. The fathers often worked as cab drivers, with computers, and in hospitals as nonprofessional staff. The fathers were more likely than the mothers to make their living by picking up various small jobs, by being paid for hauling things, for cleaning, for fixing cars, doing this or that, generally outside the Social Security and tax systems; some of the women, too, supplemented their incomes by doing such things as selling clothing in their homes, hair-dressing, or baby-sitting. Many of the children's parents were in school as well as working. Some of the women were becoming nurses or improving their English, while the men were often taking classes in computers or were in training programs for electricians. This situation changed constantly, however; some of the programs people were enrolled in were not good, and the students eventually became discouraged and quit; in other cases people had been admitted to programs without being adequately tested for their English and literacy skills, and consequently the course would turn out to be too difficult for them.

The children would often have complicated schedules because their parents were so busy. They would leave school with an uncle until their mother could get home; they would be picked up at someone else's house in the morning because their parents left home so early. Some would stay home midweek because a parent's day off occurred then. Our bus driver was the repository of all this information: He would often arrive in the morning saying something like "I went to all three houses for Jean-Christoph today and no answer; he must have gone to New York." In all this complexity, the children generally appeared to navigate quite smoothly.

Many of the parents had only a functional level of literacy in English and/or French. Some were illiterate and could only sign their names. I occasionally found that I had unwittingly put someone in a very difficult situation by casually handing over permission slips or other forms to be signed. There would be quiet consultation, perhaps as the form was read by someone else, and then painstaking work as the signature was essentially drawn. On the other hand, other parents were literate in three languages— French, Haitian Creole, and English—and had received a French-style education.

I worked at this school from 1987 to 1990. These 3 years were a time of increased immigration and much trouble for Haitians, but also one of increased national identity and activism, in Haiti as well as in U.S. cities with Haitian immigrant populations. Jean-Claude Duvalier, the son of the brutal dictator and "president for life" Papa Doc Duvalier, had been forced by a popular movement to leave the country in February 1986. This appeared to end a period of increasing poverty and despair for the Haitian people. The first elections in Haiti since 1957 were held with enormous hope in November 1987. These elections, however, were eventually halted due to violence as the Duvalierist forces, generally with the tacit support of the army, forcibly prevented people from voting. Difficult and violent years have followed in Haiti. A second election was finally held in December 1990. This election resulted in the election of Father Jean-Bertrand Aristide, a left-wing Catholic priest who won by large margins and was regarded as the champion of Haiti's poor. Although there was support for various candidates at the agency and throughout the Haitian community in my area, dismay at Aristide's ouster and at the overturning of the democratic process created some unity among the immigrant community. Many of the instructors and not a few of the clients were important people in the larger Haitian community. They were frequently speaking on radio stations and organizing rallies for the political activities that were developing during this time.

Unity and increased Haitian identity have also been aspects of the Haitian involvement with AIDS education. Haitians were considered to be particularly at risk for HIV infection. The Food and Drug Administration (FDA) passed an edict that barred Haitians from donating blood to the Red Cross because of the risk that their blood would be contaminated by HIV. Haitians demonstrated against the FDA's decision and spoke and wrote publicly explaining their disagreement. For many Haitians this was a new experience, since they had been afraid to be politically active in Haiti.

I was one of the few non-Haitian people involved at this busy place. Although we welcomed non-Haitian children at the school and non-Haitian people, where appropriate, into the adult activities, this was a place where Haitian culture and identity were central.

ATTITUDES TOWARD EDUCATION

The Haitians I know value education very highly in spite of the fact that most of them received very little education in Haiti. Haiti is variously assessed at between 80 and 90% illiterate (Clark & Purcell, 1970). Although the Haitian Constitution decrees free and compulsory public education, in reality many children are not able to attend school with any regularity. Classes typically have 45 to 60 students. The schools, especially in the rural areas, have very few materials. They are often open to the weather. Children frequently have tasks at home that take precedence over school attendance. Teachers are frequently educated only a few years beyond the class they are teaching. Until recently it has also been the case that schooling did not take place in the first language of the students—that is, Haitian schools were conducted in French. However, it is widely estimated that only 5 to 10% of the Haitian people are able to speak French, while the entire population speaks Haitian Creole.

Haitian parents are very eager for their children to take advantage of the opportunities for education that exist in the United States. Both in Haiti and in the United States, parents make enormous sacrifices to educate their children. In Haiti the best schools are usually Catholic; Haitian education, whether Catholic or not, depends largely on rote learning, on memorization and recitation. Children are expected to respect and obey their teachers in Haitian schools. The child rarely initiates interaction. The teacher's authority in the classroom is absolute. Parents expect to back the teacher up if necessary, but not to question him or her. Expecting this sort of formality, Haitian students and parents frequently are puzzled by the informality of American classrooms.

At St. George's, the family's respect for schooling was obvious in the children's dress. The children were immaculate. They were dressed formally, girls often in frilly dresses, the little boys on occasion in suits. I wore slacks, even jeans, and was rarely immaculate. I am afraid I initially thought their parents were "crazy"—why would they send children to school dressed so formally? I hesitate to think how disrespectful they must have thought my casual style and how irritated they must have been at how dirty I allowed their children to become; I simply had no ability to keep children dressed in such a manner clean. We had a lot to do to come to understand each other.

To the extent that Catholic schools here promote memorization, recitation, order, and respect for authority, they resemble the schools in Haiti, and many Haitian parents, Catholic and Protestant alike, will severely stretch their budgets to make use of them. As Haitian parents make choices for their children, other aspects of the system that they knew in Haiti continue to resonate with them. One of the most complex, and most emotional, is the language situation in Haiti.

LANGUAGE

Haitian Creole developed in Haiti in the days of slavery. It uses largely French vocabulary, but a substantially different grammar. French and Haitian Creole are not mutually intelligible. French has always been the language of the elite in Haiti, and until recently the only language used in the government and the courts, as well as the schools; Creole has been considered "franse kase," or "broken French." Contemporary work in linguistics, however, has established that Haitian Creole is not a substandard dialect of French, but a language in its own right. The grammar is complex and contains all the standard features of developed languages.

The fact that until recently most Haitians were educated in French, whether they spoke it or not, has presumably been the major reason for the high rate of illiteracy. For many Haitians, Creole is a badge of their educational failure and they have learned to be deeply ashamed of it. The attitudes of Haitian immigrants toward English, Creole, and French are highly emotional and complicated. Many people will claim that they speak French, but in reality are far from fluent in it. To speak in French, or to note an error in someone else's French, is a way to take precedence in a social situation. Réné, a friend who was getting a master's degree at an American university, told me that while he was quite comfortable speaking French with French people, he would begin sweating with anxiety when he spoke French with Haitians because an error would have been so costly to his social status.

Many parents do not want their children to speak Creole publicly. They will address their children in either French or English at home to encourage them to learn those languages instead. However, in some cases, these parents speak neither English nor French well, and so the children do not receive the necessary exposure to learn a fully complex language. Children in this situation are one source of special education referrals. In some other cases, the children did speak Creole but they had been told not to speak it in public. So, as they were learning English, they went through an exceptionally silent period, even if there were other Haitian children around; it appeared to their teachers that they had no language.

Parents who do speak Creole with their children are often ambivalent about putting their children into bilingual Creole-English programs in the public schools, since they do not regard Creole as a language of education. In day care centers in my area, Haitian-speaking teachers or teacher's aides might be hired because of the number of Haitian children enrolled but they may choose never to use Creole with the children. In fact, there will be parents who will ask them not to—they are afraid their children will not learn to speak English.

On the other hand, in many bilingual programs (such as mine), it is clear that Haitian children bring enormous linguistic resources from their native language to the task, of learning English and other learning in school (Hudicourt-Barnes, 1996; Warren & Rosebery, 1996). Despite the complex feelings many people have toward Creole in some settings, in the home and with friends it is a source of enormous pleasure and warmth. The language is full of proverbs, jokes, word-play, and metaphor. I have been a part of many fascinating conversations on the history of various expressions, on the origin of new words—people with little education become etymologists of Creole expressions. It is a language notable for its energy. There is, as well, a growing literature in Creole, and pride in its use.

LITERACY

In many ways Haiti is typical of what is frequently termed an "oral culture." Many of the Haitians that I knew were great storytellers. I spent entire evenings where people took turns telling stories and jokes, one after the other. These seemed almost always to include some acting and singing, sometimes dancing. Haitian friends tell me that among their happiest memories are the evenings when stories were told outdoors as they were growing up in Haiti. These stories were not particularly directed at them, were not what we might call children's stories. When Jean-Claude Martineau, a well-known Haitian poet and political figure, told stories to a group of children and adults, stories that in some cases centered on sexual relationships, he was asked, "but do the children understand these stories?" He replied that they did not, but that the point was that they would "come to understand them." Stories, he felt, were an ongoing part of their socialization. People participated in a variety of ways and at a variety of levels.

Many Haitian people nevertheless did find occasion to read. Some of the parents at the school were literate in some fashion in French, English, and Haitian Creole. The church services in both the Catholic and the Protestant Haitian churches were generally in Creole. It appeared that many people read Creole well enough to participate in the service and to sing the hymns. Many of the Protestants included a good deal of Bible study in their religious observance, and so many Protestant Haitians also were accustomed to reading the Bible in Creole. The children attended church and often Bible study, as well, with their parents. In the case of religious texts, the people already had some knowledge of them. In many cases these same people would say that they weren't really able to read Creole. At times they seemed to mean that they were accustomed to reading Creole only out loud, and only familiar Creole as in the church services, and so they did not consider that they were reading when they read their responses at church. Also, these texts were written in an orthography used by the churches, which has been superseded. The spelling used in current documents from Haiti and in the schools there and bilingual programs in the United States is somewhat different. Outside of church there were, in any case, few occasions to read HC.

The parents varied widely in their ability to read English. Some would occasionally prefer the American service over the Haitian service in the Catholic Church because it was faster—the Haitian Mass often lasted 2 hours on a Sunday. These people would have to read English as they participated. There were the usual requirements of reading papers from the schools, official documents, circulars in the mail. In many cases, however, the teachers at the school helped with the decoding and interpretation of these texts. Some parents were in school where they had heavy requirements for reading English; therefore, they developed adequate skills. Even in these cases storybook reading was not a typical part of family life no matter how literate the family. People I knew rarely read for pleasure, and very rarely with children. As I read storybooks to my students, I would often realize that some of the other teachers were poking their heads around my door. In passing, they had caught part of the story and wanted to know what happened. They had never heard these stories before. "What happened to Ping, after he got lost from his family?" Colette, a friend and fellow teacher at the school, asked me as I read *The Story about Ping* (Flack & Wiese, 1933). She told me that Ping's family, described in the book as including "his mother and his father and two sisters and three brothers and eleven aunts and seven uncles and forty-two cousins," was like a Haitian family and so she was particularly charmed (p. 1). The children, as they began to enjoy books at school, began to insist that their parents get them books and read to them. How this initiative will fit into family life remains to be seen.

The children in general appeared to have seen few books, held few crayons or pencils; some had never seen scissors. They seemed relatively unconcerned about print, as if it played little role in their lives. We received few written notes, and those that we did receive—for example, notes about absences, tuition owed, doctor's orders—were from a small subset of parents and were usually in French, occasionally in English. We never received anything in written Haitian Creole, although this language was used, along with English and French, within St. George's for advertisements for apartments or cars, or political rallies. To choose to write in HC was in many cases a political statement, a statement in favor of the common people and in opposition to the French-speaking elite in Haiti. There were also both church and secular newspapers written in Creole. In the school the teachers wrote for the children in both languages. Older school-age children who visited the school, however, were often surprised that people could write in Creole; they associated writing with English and school, and had evidently associated written Creole only with the sacred texts of church.

THE HAITIAN FAMILY

The Haitian family was almost always an extended one. Very rarely did I see a nuclear family occupying a house or apartment without at least one extended family member, and if they did, other family members were still an important part of everyday life. One of my colleagues, a man, lived with his wife and children, his mother, a married step-brother and the step-brother's wife and family, and some younger siblings still in school. On the other hand, Caroline, an older teacher at the school, lived alone, although her brother lived nearby. She had no children, and resisted attempts to get her to move in with anyone else.

Colette lived with her elderly father and her daughter, and always had one or more cousins, some remotely related, staying with her. Since she was a friend, I was regularly trying to help her get on top of the bureaucratic demands of her life: get her citizenship straightened out, get her father's health insurance claims completed, remortgage her house. But we were never able to achieve these goals because our attention was always diverted by another cousin who needed working papers, or needed a driver's license, and so on.

When a Haitian arrives here it is often the case that he has been helped financially by relatives in Haiti to come. He is expected to bring over other family members as part of the bargain. The connection to extended family is strong, wherever they live. Even Caroline, the woman who lived alone, when her cousin was killed in an auto accident in Haiti, immediately sent money to help pay for the boy's funeral even though she had not known him and had not been back to Haiti for 15 years. Colette, although she was not making ends meet on her salary here, paid for the education of two of her nieces in Haiti and sent money to her sisters there regularly. I constantly met people I thought of as very poor who nevertheless sent money to relatives in Haiti.

The power of the extended family created other obligations as well. I knew a young boy named Antoine whose aunt had lost a son. Antoine was sent off by his own family in Haiti to live with her and her daughter "to keep them company." He told me that he had suffered at first, but when I met him, after 5 years here, he felt useful and important and appeared to have adjusted well.

Another woman had sent for her 17-year-old nephew to join her in the United States, because "it is not safe for teenage boys in Haiti right now" (i.e., during the disorder after Aristide was overthrown). He lived with her and her already large family.

Although the father does not always live with the mother and his children, in my experience there is generally a man in the household—the mother's father or brother or cousin—and this man frequently takes some responsibility for the children in the home. The children may call him their father, and so say that they have more than one father. In Haiti, in situations where a man has children by a woman he does not live with, he is expected to give her food and/or money. Among the people that I knew, the children's father, whether he lived with the children or not, was usually very much involved with their care, frequently on a day-to-day basis. Among fathers I knew who did not live with their children, one met his young son in the stairwell of his building each morning to wait for the school bus with him because the mother had a baby upstairs that she did not want to carry down; others paid the tuition and were involved in choosing the next school. Those who did not take responsibility for their children were highly censured.

Problems often arose when a father who had married in the United States brought to this country the children he had fathered in Haiti. This is a common occurrence, since a father who emigrates to the United States has something better to offer all his children. The stepmother, however, is not always welcoming to these children. The children born here may already speak English, while the recent arrivals are older but less competent. If the recent arrival is a girl, she may be expected to do considerable work for the family. She may be expected to forgo educational opportunities and she may be poorly treated. I have been told of situations where the adults did not realize that by keeping the care-giving child home from school with the young ones, they were breaking a U.S. law. This would not have been illegal in Haiti.

Responsibility

The older children in Haitian families are generally expected to care for the younger ones. I have seen 6- and 7-year-olds with responsibility for babies and toddlers. Although many Haitians I know who have lived here for some time say that they now feel that this is too great a responsibility for such young children, it is nevertheless remarkable how well the children fulfill it. I watched a 6-year-old boy and girl playing during a parent meeting once. Soon after they began I heard the boy suggest to the girl that they go and watch his baby sister, who was sleeping in the next room. They played within sight of the sleeping child so that he could be attentive to her.

I remember waking a 3-1/2-year-old boy up from his nap next to his 2-1/2-year-old sister. Their father had come to pick them up. As I carried the little boy out of the nap room, before returning for his sister, his first remark, said with some consternation, was "I've left my little sister." [Mwen kite ti sè m.]

Frequently, when siblings were separated into different classes, the younger one would cry until reunited with the big brother or big sister, who would then with tolerant exasperation explain to me, "s/he wants me." The older child would then manage to continue playing while allowing the younger child to maintain physical contact. I am told that the children are quite likely to fight at home, but siblings were remarkably kind to each other in my sight. Nor does the responsibility of the elder end with childhood. A friend of mine, a 30-year-old woman with a husband and child, told me that she needed a new apartment, and that she was looking for one, but she really knew that her oldest sister would find it for her. This sister continued to care for her in many ways.

The ability of older children to care for younger ones was evident outside of family groups as well. The older children in my class were both competent and willing to help the younger ones with buttons, jackets, eating, going to the bathroom, and so on. I have seen a 5-year-old girl leave her meal regularly, with some exasperation but a sense of necessity, because a toddler wished her to feed him. Another child tolerated a child on her lap the entire mealtime, so that he would not cry. The boys were frequently quite as serious and reliable as the girls.

In childhood the responsibility of the elder is often compensated for by extra privileges. The practice of many American families of dividing everything equally between siblings, taking turns from the earliest days, is not so prominent among the Haitian families I know. The eldest is likely to have precedence. One younger child remembers that the eldest in her family *always* rode in the front seat of the car with her parents; there was never any turn-taking. The Haitian teachers I knew also did not generally teach sharing—they were more likely to protect the rights of the child who "got it first." As a teacher, I was upset by the lack of turn-taking as the children played. I felt at first that there was something selfish or wild about a child who could not share. It was only later that I realized this was something that American parents *teach* their children—you see children being physically helped to give another child a turn, handing over a shovel in the sandbox, for example. This training generally begins when they are still too young to understand or maybe even to do it by themselves.

Separation

For many parents it is considered an advantage to have a child born here: The child is a U.S. citizen, which is often valuable to parents with immigration difficulties themselves, and the medical care, while quite problematic in the inner-city neighborhoods where many immigrants live, is at least potentially better than that in Haiti. The child then stays with its mother while nursing, or until the mother must return to work, or until a crisis in her child-care arrangements occurs. Many families then feel that the best alternative for young children is to be cared for by family in Haiti. Others do not consider this the best alternative, but find that they have no choice due to the expense of day care. The grandmother may still be in Haiti. The grandmother is traditionally the one who brings up the children in many families, since the young adults, the parents, are the most likely to have work away from the home. Or the child may go to live with an aunt or a cousin, or a friend of the family who is available for such a task. Emmanuel's story (which I related in Chapter 1) was an example of this practice.

Joseph was perhaps fortunate in that when he came to the United States he brought his grandmother with him. He had been born in Haiti and had lived there with his grandmother while his parents, soon after his birth, came here to work. When he was old enough for kindergarten his parents sent for them both. Joseph's parents, however, were distressed that Joseph, when he arrived, continued to go to his grandmother first, rather than to them, when he needed something or was upset. Like many Haitians, these parents did not think that family feeling, love for parents, grows out of contact and intimacy. They felt that love and respect were due them because of the sacrifices they had made for Joseph while he was in Haiti. Despite the fact that he did not know them well, they believed that love and affection were due them because of the relationship itself.

I heard of another child who came here with her father when she was 3. He had family members here including sisters, so it was considered all right for him to come with the child before the mother could join them. The little girl learned to speak English and began school. After 2 years her mother arrived, with the expectation that she would resume her relationship with her daughter where she had left off. The child, however, began to have difficulties in school and became disruptive at home. The Haitian-American teacher who helped the mother deal with her child's behavior felt that the mother had not considered that the child might be angry to have been separated from her mother, however, and might have confused feelings when her mother turned up again. The mother felt that she had sacrificed for her child. She felt that her sacrifice on behalf of the child continued their relationship and could not be considered abandonment. Since they had been very close when they were together in Haiti, why were they now having difficulties?

Americans who encounter these stories of separation are typically appalled (see Rotberg, 1971). We consider it terrible to separate a child from its mother at an early age, as I did in the case of Emmanuel. The effect of these separations remains unclear, however. Haitians who have observed many such separations tell me that some children do fine, that there are ways of coping, while others may suffer greatly. It appears to them that damage to the child is not a foregone conclusion, as many Americans might assume, but neither is the practice to be taken lightly, as it sometimes is among Haitians who are accustomed to it.

Americans tend to use words like *love* very carefully, wanting to be true to some inner feeling; as parents and teachers we are likewise reluctant to force a child to say he is sorry when we believe that he is not. My sense of the way many of the Haitians I know use these terms is that they are not necessarily used to describe inner states of feeling in the same way. They are rather a part of the definition of the relationship. When one has done something wrong, it is proper to say that one is sorry. Between a parent and a child there is love—how one acts within that relationship may vary, but one does the best one can. Making sacrifices is parenting.

Discipline

The Haitian family is well known for strictness. Although there is commonly a light tone in family encounters, it is the strictness and formality that Americans tend to see and that many Haitians will choose to emphasize. Haitian people will mention that, in contrast to their view of Americans, Haitian parents typically do not joke with their children, nor wish to be friends with them. In fact, the children are generally left to themselves to play; the parents are not their children's first playmates as in so many middle-class American families. When we would go out on the playground together, I would be surprised to see the Haitian teachers generally ignoring the children and leaving them to manage by themselves. If there was one ball and many children, that was their problem. If the children had no idea what to do, looked aimless and bored, again, that was their problem. In Haiti, I am told, children would typically play in multi-age groups and with very little adult supervision or attention.

There are times in Haitian families when children may speak only when spoken to, and then they must speak in low tones and in a formal manner. In some families, it is forbidden for the child to ask direct questions or make a direct request. Haitian children, as a sign of respect, often avoid sustained eye contact with their parents, and with their teachers as well. This is of course often misunderstood by American teachers, who expect eye contact from children when they are talking to them. If the child does *not* look at you as you talk to him or her, this is generally understood in U.S. culture as being impolite. When Americans encounter these formal-appearing behaviors we often regard them as signs of a lack of close relationship between parents and children, or as signs of fear.

One day I watched a boy I knew, François, encounter an older woman in the hallway of the elementary school. He asked her if there was anything she needed, and she responded by telling him to tie his shoe. I was interested that François had been so polite and helpful to this woman, since it did not appear that he knew her, such was the formality of their manner. When I asked him, he told me that she was his mother. No wonder she had addressed his untied shoes.

Another night at a parent meeting at my school, I watched some very hungry young children after the food was set out on the table for people to serve themselves. The children carefully asked if they might have some, without making prolonged eye contact with their parents. These were happy children whose parents were devoted to them.

Unfortunately, we are equally uncomfortable with some of the behavior that does carry intimacy and closeness among Haitians. For example, Haitian mothers take more physical care of their children, and for a longer time, than Americans typically do. Children are spoonfed sometimes until past 4 years. Children may be dressed by their mothers until they are 7. In these cases we tend to feel that they are babying their children, denying them necessary independence.

As I discuss further in Chapter 4, many Haitian people think it is the family's responsibility to be strict, not to indulge their children, to make sure they act right and work hard, so that they will get ahead. Many young Haitian adults have told me that they credit their families' strictness for their own success.

There is, all the same, a complex relationship between family and community in the disciplining of children. On the one hand, Haitian parents often claim absolute authority. They do not feel at all comfortable with the idea that American institutions, such as the school or the hospital, can intervene in their family. On the other hand, here and in Haiti, the wider community is often involved in child raising. The sense of a shared value system is strong enough that, for example, people who walked into my school, on seeing a child crying or misbehaving, would speak severely to the child, invoking the mother (whom they did not know) and the mother's desires for her child's behavior. Men who grew up in Haiti remember their teenage years as times when it was really difficult to get into any trouble—

whenever they tried, people they did not know spoke to them and stopped them. It is a common experience in Haiti, as it was at St. George's, for children to be reprimanded by people they do not know. I think how shocking it would be in my neighborhood if my neighbor took it upon himself to discipline my children—it would be an enormous violation.

But in Haiti, the parents are not expected to raise their children without help. A Haitian woman made this point when she told me about taking her 4-year-old nephew to the beach in this country. The boy was misbehaving, kicking sand on other people's blankets. She said she was embarrassed as she tried to control him since she clearly understood that she was being held responsible by the people around her. She felt that in Haiti people would have been more sympathetic; "you've got a hard job," she imagined that they would have said. She would not have felt solely responsible for the child's behavior.

Another child, a teenager, in the Haitian community here was caught stealing in school. His teacher made an appointment to visit the family to tell them what had happened. When she arrived the boy was there with his father, and many of his father's friends as well. She was invited to go ahead and explain. Then all the father's friends joined the father in reprimanding the boy and pressuring him to act right. At parent meetings at my school, parents would often ask in front of everyone assembled how their child was doing. In both these examples, I would have expected this information to be saved for a more private interview.

It is also not unusual, on the other hand, for people to intervene on the side of the child if they feel that the parents are being overly harsh. In Haiti, if a child is being beaten, a neighbor or relative, hearing the cries, may come to plead on his behalf. Both the support of the community and the constraint of neighborly intervention are of course less constant in urban immigrant communities than they were in Haiti. One can imagine the greater stress this change places on the customary family ways of raising children.

CONCLUSION

In the next chapters I will explore how the attitudes toward schooling that my students came with from their families interacted with my attitudes and the attitudes of the school. The children arrived prepared for school in ways I did not know and to which I was not accustomed. Looking back on the years I spent at St. George's, I think I was very fortunate to be a minority of one, the outsider. Here, because my accustomed ways of doing things in the classroom were not familiar to these children, or to the other teachers, I was forced to reconsider my beliefs, to try to understand what lay behind them, and to work to hear the children and their parents better.

Chapter 4

"BECAUSE YOU LIKE US":
THE LANGUAGE OF CONTROL

In this chapter I will discuss the process I went through in learning to control a class of young Haitian children. For teachers who do not share their culture, Haitian children are often difficult to control. This was becoming a recognized problem, both from the point of view of American teachers that I knew, and from the point of view of the Haitian parents at my school and in the larger community. This chapter is an account of the many conversations I had, among people from a variety of backgrounds, all concerned with the words we use and the things we say, in the family and in the school, when we ask children to behave.

THE PROBLEM

Since I had many years of experience teaching in this arena programs for children with behavior problems, I did not expect to have problems when I came to this school. I was used to being both tough and understanding with young children and I thought I knew what to do. However, I had major problems. The children ran me ragged. In the friendliest, most cheerful and affectionate manner imaginable, my class of 4-year-olds followed their own inclinations rather than my directions in almost everything. I would claim that I am not a person who needs to have a great deal of control, but in this case I had very little, and I did not like it.

I tried many of my standard practices. I would praise the child who happened to be doing what I wished in the hearing of the others. This, however, would often lead to the singled-out child's becoming extremely uncomfortable. I repeatedly offered explanations and consequences for their behavior. Although there were exceptions, on a typical day I had very little sense of being in control.

My difficulties increased when I looked around at the other classrooms at my school. There, I was uncomfortably aware, the other teachers—all Haitian women with far less education and training than I—ran orderly classrooms of children who, in an equally affectionate and cheerful manner, did follow directions and kept the confusion to a level that I could have tolerated. The problem, evidently, did not reside in the children, since the Haitian teachers managed them well enough. Where then did it reside? What was it that the Haitian teachers did that I did not?

I tried asking them. Colette told me I loved the children too much. I asked her if she didn't love the children. She agreed that she and the other teachers did love the children, but she said I let them know it. I asked her if the children didn't know that she loved them. She agreed that they did. We could not figure out what it was I needed to know.

At this time I was also one of two instructors for a course in child development, offered for Haitian people who wished to find jobs in day care centers. This group recognized the problem on their own terms. As part of the course, they were all interning in various day care centers and preschools—some with me at St. George's, but the majority in other centers. Many of the latter were extremely concerned about behavior problems. What they told me and told each other was that many of the children in their centers were behaving very poorly; many felt that this was particularly true of the Haitian children. They felt that the way in which they were being instructed to deal with the children's behavior was not effective. One woman explained to me that when she was hit by a 4-year-old, she was instructed to acknowledge the anger he must be feeling, then to explain to him that he could not hit her. She told me that from her point of view, this was the same as suggesting politely, "Why don't you hit me again?"

When I talked with Haitian parents at St. George's I heard similar complaints. From the point of view of many of the people I talked with, the behavior tolerated in their neighborhood schools was disrespectful; the children were allowed to misbehave. A common refrain in these conversations was "We're losing a generation of children"—the young children here now, not brought up first in Haiti, were not being brought up with the same values. However, when I first asked for specific advice about things I might do to manage the children better, the teachers and I could never get to any behaviors of mine that I could try to change.

I took my problem to the BTRS, not really expecting much help since this problem seemed outside normal curriculum areas. In this case, I was encouraged to approach my problem by discovering what it was that the Haitian teachers said to the children in situations where directions were being given. Like most people inside a culture or a system of values and beliefs, the Haitian teachers and parents could not tell me what they said and why, but perhaps I could discover it, and then discuss it with them.

The BTRS has also come to believe that an important part of a research project is researching where the research question comes from in one's own life: why it seems important; what its value is to the teacher-researcher. In many cases, this is a matter of investigating one's own socialization. Thus

I began to explore my own beliefs and practices in regard to what I considered proper children's behavior and this part of the process became a very important aspect of this work as well.

TEXTS

I began to collect texts—that is, I began to write down what the Haitian teachers said to the children in situations where their behavior was at issue. I will call these "control" situations. I ignored situations where the teachers made no explanations and only said something like "No" or "Stop." I concentrated instead on those instances in which the directions that a teacher gave were supported by some additional information. By choosing the longer texts, I thought I would be able to see more of the values and intentions behind what they said and why it worked. These texts then became one focus of the child development course, as well as of my work in the seminar. I am going to present a few of these texts that I consider typical, and then share some of the responses and the thinking engendered by these texts among the various people with whom I shared them.

I present first Clothilde's account of an event at her day care center. Clothilde is a middle-aged Haitian woman, and one of the students in the child development course. She has a great deal of experience with children—from raising her own and from caring for other people's—and many of her classmates turn to her for advice. In the text below, she has been complaining to me about the behavior of the Haitian children in the day care center where she is student teaching. She thinks that the American teachers are not controlling them adequately.

One day, as Clothilde arrives at her school, she watches a teacher telling a Haitian child to go into her classroom, that she cannot stay alone in the hall. The child refuses and eventually kicks the teacher. Clothilde has had enough. She asks the director to give her all the Haitian kids right away. The following is the text of what she told me she said to the children:

Clothilde: Does your mother let you bite?
Kids: No.
Clothilde: Does your father let you punch kids?
Kids: No.
Clothilde: Do you kick at home?
Kids: No.
Clothilde: You don't respect anyone, not the teachers who play with you
    or the adults who work upstairs. You need to respect adults—even
    people you see on the streets. You are taking good ways you learn at

home and not bringing them to school. You're taking the bad things you learn at school and taking them home. You're not going to do this anymore. Do you want your parents to be ashamed of you?

According to Clothilde, the Haitian children have been well behaved ever since. Other Haitian teachers with whom I have shared this text have said, yes, that was what the children needed. However, they also said that Clothilde will have to renew her speech, because the children won't remain well behaved forever without a new dose.

The next text involves an incident at my school. Colette was reprimanding a group of children who had been making a lot of noise while their teacher was trying to give them directions:

Colette: When your mother talks to you, don't you listen?
Children: Yes.
Colette: When your mother says, go get something, don't you go get it?
Children: Yes.
Colette: When your mother says, go to the bathroom, don't you go?
Children: Yes.
Colette: You know why I'm telling you this. Because I want you to be good children. When an adult talks to you, you're supposed to listen so you will become a good person. The adults here like you, they want you to become good children.

Finally, we have Jérémie's father speaking to him. Jérémie is a very active 5-year-old, and the staff had asked his father for help in controlling his behavior.

Father: Are you going to be good? [Jérémie nods at each pause.] Are you going to listen to Miss Cindy? Are you going to listen to Miss Colette? Because they like you. They love you. Do it for me. Do it for God. Do you like God? God loves you.

DISCUSSION OF THE TEXTS

It seems that the content and the form of these texts are different from what I, or many American teachers, would have said in the same circumstance. I shared these texts, as well as other texts and observations, with many people, parents and teachers, Haitian and American. I asked them to reflect with me on what these differences were and on what the underlying values and intentions were. The following is a blend of their observations and self-reflection, as well as my own. Although I am trying to distill these conversations in order to identify "typical" practices of Haitian or American teachers, the sense of these discussions was certainly not that all American or all Haitian teachers are the same.

The Haitian preschool teachers had clear insights into behavior characteristics of American teachers. Clothilde commented that the American teachers she knows frequently refer to internal states of the children and interpret their feelings for them, for example, "You must be angry," "It's hard for you when your friend does that," and so on. Clothilde pointed out to me that in her speech she makes no reference to the children's emotions, nor do the Haitian teachers I have observed do this as a rule.

Rose, another Haitian teacher, also commented that American teachers often make reference to particular factors in the child's situation that, in the teacher's opinion, may have influenced his behavior. For example, Michel, whose mother had left him, was often told that the teachers understood that he missed his mother, but that, nevertheless, he needed to share his toys. Or, when a child pushes or pinches another child sitting right next to her, many teachers will suggest that if the child does not like people to sit so close, she should say so rather than pinch them to make them move. Rose felt, and in my observation I concurred, that Haitian teachers do not often do this. Colette suggested further that if she were concerned about an individual child and his particular problems, instead of articulating for him the difficulties in his life, her goal would be "to make him feel comfortable with the group." If he were misbehaving, she would say, "You know I'm your friend," and then remind him, "we don't do that." In fact, I have seen her do exactly that many times to excellent effect.

These examples suggest to me a difference in focus between the American and the Haitian teachers. It seems that American teachers characteristically are concerned with making a connection with the individual child, helping the child to articulate feelings and problems. Clothilde and Colette, on the other hand, and the many Haitian people I spoke with and observed, emphasize the group in their control talk. They articulate the values and responsibilities of group membership. For example, as we have seen, both American and Haitian teachers make reference to families, but in different ways. American teachers are likely to mention particular characteristics of a child's family, characteristics that are specific to that family and are seen as perhaps responsible for the child's actions. The Haitian teachers emphasize instead what the families have in common. The families do not differ in their desire that the children respect adults, that the children behave properly, and that their behavior not shame them. The children's answers, in the cases where they are given in unison as in Clothilde's text above, present a vivid enactment of the sort of unity this approach at times engenders.

Another difference we noted is the use of consequences. American teachers typically present the particular consequences of a piece of misbehavior. For example, I often say something like "He's crying because you hit him," or "If you don't listen to me, you won't know what to do." Haitian teachers are less likely to differentiate among particular kinds of misbehavior; they are more likely to condemn them all, not in terms of their consequences but simply as examples of "bad" behavior. Clothilde is typical of the Haitian teachers in that the immediate consequences are not made explicit; she does not explain why she is against biting or punching. She refers to such behavior as "bad" and explains to the children the consequences of bad behavior in general—shame for the family, in this case. Jérémie's father simply tells Jérémie to be good, to be good for those who love him. Colette too tells the children to be good because the people who like them want them to be good. I have heard other Haitian teachers refer to the impression that bad behavior would create in a passer-by, or to the necessity of modeling good behavior for younger children. But specific consequences of particular acts are rarely mentioned, a clear difference from American teachers.

In the Haitian texts, one has the impression that the children share the adult's understanding of what bad behavior is. Clothilde's series of rhetorical questions—for example, "Do your parents let you kick?"—is an example of the form many Haitian teachers adopt when addressing children about their behavior. The children understand their role without difficulty; they repeat the expected answers in choral unison. The choice of this form, that is, questions to which the answer is assumed, emphasizes the fact that the children already know that their behavior is wrong.

In the American control situation, on the other hand, the child often appears to be receiving new information. If there is a consensus about behavior—certain behavior is bad, certain other behavior is good—we don't present it this way. Americans frequently explain the consequences of particular actions as if we were trying to convince the child that there was a problem with the behavior. As presented in school, misbehavior is considered wrong not because of anything inherent in it, but because of its particular consequences, or perhaps because the behavior stems from feelings that the child has failed to identify and control.

These differences, as I came to recognize them, seemed significant enough to account for some of the difficulties I had been experiencing in my classroom. But what to do about them?

PRACTICE

With the overwhelming evidence that these children were used to a kind of control talk other than what I had been providing, I began to adopt some of the style of the Haitian teachers. This was not initially easy for me to do, contradicting as it did my own socialization. I assume that I was not very good at it. I am sure that I had no idea of the nuances. One time, as I reprimanded them, I realized that the children were worried: "OK, OK," they said defensively. I believe they thought I was very angry. I realized then that I had never seen them react in this worried way with the Haitian teachers. This was an ironic realization, since I had been initially resistant to the Haitian teachers' style because I thought they were scaring the children.

As I have developed a more or less stable mélange of styles, including some of my old ways with my newly acquired ones, my control in the classroom has improved significantly. I have found as well that I love trying on this Haitian way. I was struck by an experience I had one day when I was reprimanding one boy for pinching another child. I was focusing, in the Haitian manner, on his prior, indisputable knowledge that pinching was simply no good. I also used my best approximation of the facial expression and tone of voice that I see the Haitian teachers use in these encounters. I can tell when I have it more or less right because of the way the children pay attention. As I finished this particular time, the other children, who had been rapt, all solemnly thanked me. They were perhaps feeling in danger of being pinched and felt that I had at last been effective. This solemn sort of response, however, has occurred a few other times. Their solemnity in particular gives me the sense that these situations are very important to them.

Perhaps one final anecdote may suggest the way in which I came to see this importance. One day I was angrily reprimanding the children about their failure to wait for me while crossing the parking lot:

Cindy: Did I tell you to go?
Kids: No.
Cindy: Can you cross this parking lot by yourselves?
Kids: No.
Cindy: That's right. There are cars here. They're dangerous. I don't want you to go alone. Why do I want you to wait for me, do you know?

"Yes," says Kenthea, "because you like us."
Although I was following the Haitian form—rhetorical questions with

"No" answers—I had been expecting a final response based on the American system of cause and effect, something like, "because the cars are dangerous." Kenthea, however, although she understands perfectly well the dangers of cars to small children, does not expect to use that information in this kind of an interaction. Then what is she telling me? One thing that she is saying, which is perhaps what the solemn children meant too, is that from her point of view, there is intimacy in this kind of talk. This is certainly the feeling that I get from these experiences. I feel especially connected to the children in these instances in which I seem to have gotten it right.

American teachers generally think of reprimands—particularly of young children who are just learning to control their behavior—as put-downs. We are reluctant to give them. American preschool teachers, in particular, will take great pains to avoid saying "No" or "Don't." Research in this area generally reflects this attitude as well. Boggs (1985) for example, describes as an anthropologist the rather authoritarian style Hawaiian parents employ in disciplining their children. His work in education is intended to allow what he calls "mainland" teachers to make their classrooms more culturally familiar to Hawaiian children and to make use of, in particular, culturally familiar patterns of interaction in educating these children. And yet, even as he recognizes the importance of the classroom management problems that Hawaiian children pose to mainland teachers, he does not consider making use of the Hawaiian style of control. At one point he even mentions that a child is misbehaving in a way he never would if the Hawaiian class-room aide were present. But evidently the sort of management that the aide represents is not within the realm of possible pedagogical behavior, as Boggs sees it, since it is never mentioned again.

The belief that the use of reprimands and the imposition of authority are detrimental to young children is in significant contrast to what I found in my classroom. One thing I believe I learned is that there are situations in which reprimands are confirming, in which they strengthen relationships and in a sense define them for the child. This seems to have been the case for Kenthea above. Such an opportunity may be lost when we go to great lengths to avoid actually telling a child that she is wrong, that there is such a thing as "bad" behavior and that her behavior is not acceptable in her community.

When we look at the difference between the ways in which things are done at home and at school and the negative consequences that may result from these mismatches for children coming from minority cultural back-grounds, the area of misbehavior and the way it is responded to seems particularly important because it affects so directly the nature of the relation-ship between child and teacher.

THE WIDER CONTEXT

I was not unaware when I began my investigation that this subject was a hotbed of disagreement: Americans perceive Haitians as too severe, both verbally and in their use of physical punishment; on the other hand, Haitians often perceive American children as being extraordinarily fresh and out of control. Haitian immigrant parents here are both ashamed and defiantly supportive of their community's disciplinary standards and methods. In order to represent the views of the Haitians I was speaking with independent of my process of understanding, I asked them—after they had heard my interpretations—to reflect again on our two cultures.

People of course differed in many ways in their points of view. Yet, everybody emphasized a sense of having been very "protected" in Haiti, of having been safe there both from getting into serious trouble and from harm. This sense of being protected was largely based on their understanding that their entire extended family and many people in the wider community as well were involved in their upbringing. Among Haitians in the United States, people pointed out, families are smaller and less extended. The community, while tight in many ways, is more loosely held together than in Haiti. This change in social structure was bemoaned by the people I spoke with, most especially in reference to bringing up children. The sense that this generation of children, particularly those "born here," are very much at risk is attributed in part to this change.

Yet, everyone I spoke with also recalled some pain in their growing up, pain they relate to the respect and obedience they were required to exhibit to all adults, which at times conflicted with their own developing desire to state their opinion or make their own choices. This pain, although identified as such, was nevertheless not to be discarded lightly. For many people religious values underlie these twin issues of respect and obedience; respect for parents and other adults is an analogue for respect and obedience to God and God's law.

Many people seemed to agree with the ambivalence expressed by the Haitian lawyer and mother who told me that, while she had suffered as a child because of the uncompromising obedience and respect demanded by her family, she continued to see respect as a value she needed to impart to her children. However, she suggested to me: "There must be many other ways to teach respect." She was one of many Haitians who told me of instances where a child from a poor family, a child with neither the clothes nor the supplies for school, had succeeded eventually in becoming a doctor or a lawyer. In these accounts, as in hers, it is in large measure the strictness of the family that is regarded as the source of the child's accomplishment, rather than the talent or the power of the individual.

Presumably, in all societies there is some tension between individual and community. In these accounts is some suggestion of the form this tension takes within Haitian culture. For my part, I am struck and troubled by the powerful individualism underlying the approach I characterize as typical of myself and many American teachers. It appears that Americans do speak as if something like the child's "enlightened self-interest" were the ultimate moral guidepost. In comparison with the language used by the Haitian teachers, there is very little emphasis on shared values, on a moral community.

The process of exploring my own behavior and beliefs about this topic was a crucial part of this piece of research. I had been trained to handle behavior in certain ways, but this training was based on deep cultural assumptions. This process helped me perceive the behavior of the Haitian teachers, who at first seemed to me to be too strict and without empathy or connection, as sensible and full of moral value and intentions; on the other hand, what had seemed familiar and natural to me—my own values and practices—became subject to examination.

Chapter 5

LEARNING THE ABCs: THE SHADOW CURRICULUM

When you live in the classroom as teachers do, you are in a position to see the richness and resonance of the social life that children bring to their classroom tasks. But you may wonder, as I have, how their social intentions interact with their learning. Do their social goals support their learning or derail it, or are they irrelevant altogether to the academic curriculum?

My Haitian students brought to school a desire to make friends and to feel comfortable away from their families. What they didn't bring was much experience of reading and writing. Here I present what I learned about interactions between, on the one hand, friendship and love in the world of my preschoolers, and, on the other hand, their acquisition of concepts of print.

THE PROBLEM

I am not prepared to say what their home experience with print was, but, as discussed in Chapter 2, it is well known that literacy rates in Haiti are extremely low. Among the parents of these children, I was aware of various levels of literacy: Some were functionally literate in either French or English; some, however, could only sign their names; some couldn't even do that; a few had received a French-style education in Haiti and were highly literate in three languages. Still, as I mentioned earlier, even among these highly literate Haitians it was not customary to read stories to young children. People told stories, but did not read them. Nor were the children typically given paper and pencil at home to play at writing.

Their parents were nevertheless concerned that they become literate, but many of them felt that this was the school's job. The view of literacy espoused by many of the parents contained an emphasis on memorizing and copying. They were eager, for example, for their children to write the alphabet, particularly in a mature-looking handwriting, but they were less impressed that the children could comment on storybooks, draw stories, or pretend to read.

The signs of early literacy that I was accustomed to seeing were, not surprisingly, not evident in my classroom that year (Bissex, 1980; Clay, 1975, 1992; Ferreiro & Teberosky, 1982; Goodman, 1986; Harste, Woodward, & Burke, 1984). The children did not, for example, know how to hold a book; they did not know letter names nor did they try to write them; they were not accustomed to drawing; their early scribbles did not distinguish between letter-like forms and drawings. In fact they did not seem familiar with print at all.

Recognizing that these children were starting in a different place than other groups I had taught, I began to collect the children's interaction with letters—that is, I audiotaped them at the writing table and made notes on my interactions with them around print. I tried to have a record of everything that happened that seemed related to print. I didn't do this because I thought it would be important to others, or as a diagnostic tool, or to gain a sense of where they were. I did it because I knew I was going to be teaching them about letters and text, and I wanted to see in detail what was happening as I did so. It has become a principle of BTRS research that you can't fix something until you understand it, until you have explored the details of the interactions, what was said and done and by whom. I needed to see my students as they made meaning out of what I was showing them.

As I watched and taped and scribbled my field notes, I soon realized that a good deal of what I was observing was not familiar. It was not what they weren't able to do that surprised me—there are many accounts in the literature of children from less literate backgrounds that explore this—but what they *were* doing; this I had not seen described before and it began to fascinate me. Putting together what I heard on the audiotapes and what I noted, discussing it with others, I began to see that, while I had my curriculum on the subject, they were also hard at work developing theirs. Mine was based on what I thought was important about letters and writing, and the children's, not surprisingly, was based on what they thought. I will call theirs the "shadow curriculum" because I think it is usually relegated to the shadows. In the following sections, I will describe both my curriculum and the shadow curriculum and then discuss what I came to see as the value of the interaction between them.

MY CURRICULUM

Like many preschool teachers, I do not operate with a hard-and-fast curriculum the way some elementary school teachers do. I have goals in mind, and activities and areas developed to promote the goals, but nothing is rigid. I don't, for example, insist that the children spend time writing or working with print. Nevertheless, these activities are something I clearly value. I set up a writing area with paper, letter stencils, markers, pencils, even pens if they ask for them, everyday. I tend to be available at the writing table more than at other areas. But I am not available anywhere very often. I am busy—the children must also rely on each other.

As I design the space and the activities of the preschool day, I consider two related but separable areas of young children's concepts of print: (1) what you can do with print, that is, the functions of print in the world, and (2) what a letter has to do with a word. In terms of functions, I am concerned that they understand that print can tell a story and get a message to mother, can indicate the days of the week, can label an area the Art Corner, can label a cubby or a picture as your own, can help people remember things. Consequently I label many things in the classroom as well as their cubbies and drawings. I offer to write for them. We occasionally write letters or cards to various people.

In understanding how print works, what the letters do in words, a crucial early step is the recognition that it is the print that tells people what to say when they are reading—that when they read storybooks it is not the pictures they are reading. In various ways, both implicit and explicit, I try to bring this to the children's attention. I expect that in their early attempts to determine the relation between letters and words they will make various hypotheses, some of them idiosyncratic, many of them standard. Teachers and researchers have observed children who believed that the first letters of their names belonged to them and them alone, or that one could start writing one's name at either end. I have known children who felt that all names had to be the same length, and some for whom a big sister's name should be longer than their own, children who felt that if you have written the first "e" in Steven there can't possibly be a reason for another one. And so on.

I expect that these hypotheses will be continually reanalyzed and corrected by the child in light of his or her continuing experience with print. I see my job as making sure that the experiences are there. I do this by explicit teaching of facts ("No, that is not your name yet. You need a Y at the end"); by drawing their attention to contradictions in their theories ("Only girls can have Ss, Suzanne? What about Steven and here's an S in Rubenson"); and by doing lots of reading and writing. At the same time I really value the kind of thinking that goes on in these hypotheses, right or wrong. I see it as logical thinking, as analysis.

However, these children, as I said, did not share my experience with print. I wrote their names on their cubbies; they watched solemnly, but still used any cubby one that was convenient. They knew no letter names. They couldn't recognize their own written names. When I wrote Rubenson's name for him he accepted it. But when he realized I could write any name that I wanted, he was amazed. "You know how to mark them all?" he asked. Emmanuel was making a picture of an apple. As he colored the apple, his crayon went through the paper. "Oh, a worm ate it, look," he laughed. I laughed too, then told him I would write that on his paper. As I began to write "A worm ate the apple," Emmanuel looked appalled. "What are you doing?" he demanded. He had no idea.

Kenthea told me tearfully that she didn't know how to write her mother's name. I began to make an M, telling her meanwhile that her mother's name was Marie and it began with an M. She said "No, no. Eyes." After a moment's confusion, during which Kenthea made no effort to explain but stubbornly stared up at me, I realized she wanted a circle for the face, and she would put in the eyes. It was a circle she meant when she had said "Her mother's name." She subsequently demanded circles for each member of her family. "What about Peter? Where's Josy, and my uncle?" and after adding the eyes to each, she was satisfied.

Yet these children were fascinated by letters. They spent entire mornings at the table where I put our various writing and drawing tools. They helped each other learn to match letters until every child could do all 26, even the youngest, who was not yet 3. They kept their papers with them while they did other things. Children copied print from everywhere, indiscriminately, from the bottoms of toy cars, from zoo posters, from anything they saw, and brought it over for me to read. I often found myself reading such phrases as "Manufactured in Taiwan" and wondering if there was any value in responding to all their requests. It sometimes seemed they might be testing me to see if I really could read anything.

During the course of the year, at varying rates, they learned to write their names, to recognize each other's names, to name and match letters, to recognize STOP and EXIT, to say the ABCs. They came to understand that it is the print that you read, not the pictures in a book. One child began an invented spelling.

Emmanuel perhaps came the farthest; he had begun by asking me what I was doing as I wrote a sentence on his picture. He came in one day with a 3 × 5 card on which he had written (I believe with his kindergarten broth-er's help) MOMYABDE. This was intended to be a forged permission slip. The physical therapist played baseball with the children and Emmanuel wanted to work with her; for this he needed a permission slip. Clearly there was still information he needed in order to successfully forge his mother's signature, but he was well on his way to many crucial literacy skills.

In some sense I see all of this as what I taught them. They learned it, but it was my agenda. Yet I had never experienced such determination to learn. I want to suggest that the motivation resided largely in the shadow curriculum, their curriculum.

THE SHADOW CURRICULUM

The following are notes from my journal and transcriptions from audiotapes made at the writing table. They are instances of the shadow curriculum, uses of print that were outside of my plans and expectations.

Note 1

Jean calls Suzanne whenever he finds an *S* among the letters. "Suzanne, your *S*." She obediently goes to him each time she is called and looks at the letter he is indicating, then returns to wherever she is playing.

Note 2

Jean-Marc spells his name: *J* for Jean-Marc, *E* for Emmanuel, *A* for André, *N* for Natalie—and then he stops, he cannot go further since he knows no one whose name begins with *M*.

Note 3

Tiny Tatie, not yet 3 years old, never says a word and never comes to circle where we read the names and talk a little about letters. I am amazed to discover that she has been walking around the classroom all morning with two fingers in the shape of a *T*. When asked what she's doing, she says, "It's me," and continues silently to parade her *T* around the classroom.

Note 4

We are writing with magnetic letters when we realize that there are no *T*s. Earlier some children had been coloring capital *T*s and *J*s. One of these children suggests that we look for the magnetic *T* in Tatie's cubby, since she had taken all the colored *T*s and put them there. And there we find all the *T*s.

Note 5

Suzanne's mother comes into the classroom. Tatie solemnly hands her a paper on which she has colored a huge *S*. Suzanne's mother looks baffled, as I am too until it occurs to me that Tatie has handed the mother her daughter's letter. Tatie then shows Suzanne's mother her *T*.

Note 6

Kenthea is painting. I come to write her name on her painting for her. She has me add her brother's name, her sister's name, and her mother and father's and her uncle's (who also lives with her). As the year progresses she continues to do this in one form or another.

Note 7

Giles is just 4 years old. He had learned to write his whole name. This day Giles is making his *G*, announcing it as he goes. "Cindy, I make my *G*." He cuts the paper on which he has written, carefully avoiding the *G*, and parades around the classroom saying, "I no cut my *G*." He repeats the process, making more *G*s and not cutting them many times this morning, each time announcing to me and the world, "Cindy, I no cut my *G*." Finally I find myself saying to him, "No, Giles, I see, you take good care of your *G*" as if he were carrying a doll around instead of a letter. Giles later appears with a *P* for Pierre and an *J* for Jean-Marc, his two best buddies. He doesn't cut them either, as he tells us all. Next he makes an *S* for Steven, whom he does not like. "I cut Steven's *S*," he announces in a dire tone.

Note 8

Giles has been following me around today with his drawings. First he brings me one with a smiling face. He hides it behind his back, saying, "Cindy, I have a surprise for you." He pulls it out, saying, "Look, boy so happy. Write boy so happy" all the while smiling himself. I write "Boy so happy" on his picture. He then goes off and creates another. When he returns, again he hides this one behind his back. He then pulls it out, saying, "Look, boy so sad," looking sad himself. He repeats the pattern several times, each time matching his face to the drawing. Sometimes I write for him, other times he doesn't give me time. He appears thrilled with this activity. He is rapidly creating drawings, naming them "Boy so happy" or "Boy so sad," matching the expression on his face to the drawing, and then going on to the next. Finally, as he is creating a "Boy so happy" picture, his marker slips on the mouth, and it looks sad instead. Giles had gotten as far as "Look, Cindy, boy so hap" when the marker slips. As he looks at the now downturned mouth, he switches, both what he is saying and his own expression. "Boy so hap, sad," he says, suddenly mournful.

Note 9

When I leave my position at the school the children are all instructed by their various teachers to write their names on a good-bye card for me. In addition and without instruction, many of them bring me pieces of paper on which they have written my letter, C.

Let me explain what I see in these data by first looking at individual children and then drawing some more general conclusions.

Jean

In Note 1, Jean and Suzanne are playing together—the activity is keeping track of Suzanne's Ss. There is another girl whose name begins with S, as Jean well knows, but she and Jean are not particularly close, so it is Suzanne that he calls to him each time he can find an S. Print is part of being friends with Suzanne, and being friends with Suzanne is a way to use print.

Jean-Marc

The way Jean-Marc spells, using everyone's name, becomes typical for the classroom. All the children who can, identify the letters of their name in this way. I initially try to break them of the habit, assuming that they have the mistaken impression that you can own letters, that your letter is yours and yours alone. I am, therefore, always telling them that it is not really Tatie's T, for example. Other children and other words also have Ts. We always observe when more than one child's name begins with the same letter. The children accept what I say, and learn that turtle begins with T and that stop has a T. However, nothing breaks them of this way of spelling, until I finally became charmed by it myself. Again, print and friendship proceed together.

Tatie

Tatie, the youngest in the class, tries to keep all the Ts—coloring papers, magnetic Ts, cut-out letters—in her cubby. She knows that she shares T at least with Teo, another child at the school. She is a very silent child, although obviously aware. In Note 5, Tatie has used the *S* and her *T* to greet, to make some sort of social connection with, Suzanne's mother at a point where she is still not willing to talk.

Kenthea

Kenthea, in Note 6, is typical of a number of the children who rarely wanted their names written alone. They usually wanted their families included, although sometimes friends take their place. She is also the child who, earlier in the year, wanted circles for her whole extended family so that she could fill in the eyes. Although she is dropped off at school each day by her uncle, who leaves after a quick good-bye, in some sense she does not come to school without her whole family. If she is going to learn to write then she will write all their names. When she draws, she draws them all too.

Giles

Giles is an actor in his text of letters, just the way many young children are in their early attempts at written text (Dyson, 1992).

In Note 8, Giles demonstrates a slightly novel perspective on drama and representation. His facial expression changes when the face he is drawing changes, even when he did not intend that change. Giles appears unsure who is in control, the representation or the author. The representation is surely affecting him, but he does not appear to be sure that he can affect it. Giles is a wonderfully dreamy child, and here he seems to be operating in a space of some tension between actual and possible worlds, between the real and the imaginary.

In Note 7, he places his own letter on the public stage by announcing the letter and his care for it. He then includes his two friends in the circle of his care, and acts out his opposite feeling for another member of the group. He uses letters to comment on his connections with, and feelings for, his friends. At first, as Giles talks to me about not cutting his *G*, I respond by commenting on what a good *G* he has drawn, and by suggesting that he complete his name. Giles, however, keeps repeating that he hadn't cut his *G*. He does not appear satisfied until I finally say, "Yes, Giles, I see, you take good care of your *G*." At that point he goes on to make other letters and act on them. What is behind such persistence?

My final response, the one he accepts, is not a response to his developing literacy. Rather, as I recognize much later from listening to myself on the audiotape, "You take good care of your *G*" is the sort of response I make when children are playing in the house corner with dolls: There the children often point out to me the care they take of their dolls, and I generally let them know that I recognize that they are indeed careful and responsible. In these conversations, my understanding is that we are making reference to the care that the child receives at home, and the ability that the child has to carry that care with him, to take care of himself, away from home. When I talk with preschoolers about the way they can care for their dolls, I am reminding them on some level that they can remember their mothers and the nurturance and comfort of home, and that, as they play in this way, that memory can keep them warm while they are at school. Giles has moved us into this symbolic territory (Braun & Lasher, 1978; Morton, 1992)—territory that he and I know and love—but that I don't expect to encounter in the midst of his work on printing.

SOCIAL AND INTELLECTUAL LIVES

The model I had of how children acquire concepts of print generally derived from a sense that experiences with print are data from which children induce the logic of the rules for reading and writing (Bissex, 1980; Clay, 1992; Clay & Cazden, 1990; Ferreiro and Teberosky, 1982). I knew a child, for example, who had a hypothesis that to write about a big house you need more letters than to write about a small house. Her progression to a more accurate understanding was prompted by the recognition that her big sister's name has fewer letters than her own. I saw my students' development as the result of hypotheses that are challenged by encounters with new evidence. Learning in this area took place in a quasi-scientific context, a context that privileges logic and analysis. The motivation to learn is the motivation to solve a logical puzzle. This model perhaps describes accurately some part of the children's learning, yet, looking at my students, it is clear that for them such a model leaves a great deal of their learning and their motivation out.

My students had some very important goals. They were working on leaving their families and finding friendship and security in the world of their friends. And the ABCs were a part of the process. They used print as a way to develop and to think about friendship and to hold on to their feeling for their parents, in both the real world and in imagined worlds. Let us look at the accounts from my class from this perspective.

Kenthea, for example, is representing her world with letters, or earlier with circles for faces. As she signs her papers with the names of her entire family, she places herself as part of her social world, as do the various spellers. They do not represent themselves as standing alone. Jean, as he continually shows Suzanne the Ss he finds, and Tatie, as she connects with Suzanne's mother, use letters in a slightly different way, not to represent their community but to enact it. The letters seem to be part of an exchange that develops relationships. Jean is making friends with Suzanne, as Tatie is with Suzanne's mother. On the good-bye card the children were giving me something that would help me remember them, their names, but by also giving me my C, again they enact our connection.

Giles has more complex intentions. With the happy and sad faces, Giles is at first depicting himself in an imagined situation; then, when his hand slips and a happy face becomes a sad one, it is the representation that appears to determine reality—life imitates art. In Giles's drama with letters, he begins by acting out with me the meaning he sees in community, the nurturant "good care." Then, using this, he goes on to construct his social network with letters. By publicly announcing that he takes "good care" of the letters of his friends, and by announcing his contrasting desire to cut Steven's S, he places his interpretation of friendship in front of his classmates; it is a story of friends and enemies. Giles appears to be presenting reality— who his friends are and who his enemies are—and, in the publicness of his interpretation, he is also affecting it. I would guess that he feels like a storyteller as he goes on, a particularly artful one, as his drama unfolds with his letter-props. He is engrossed and determined. Letters are part of the drama of life, of leaving home, of nurturant care, of finding friends and finding enemies, and naming them as such.

Another teacher-researcher, Karen Gallas (1992) has documented instances where children's imagined worlds, shared with others, then make a difference in the actual world. In Gallas's account, children in her first grade, by including particular classmates as characters in their made-up stories, appear to in fact create stronger relationships with those children. Friendships, once imagined, become possible. In this case, the children's fiction is affecting their community in the actual world. The shadow curriculum supported the children in the endeavor of novelists—to represent their world and then, by means of these representations, to affect the world, to evaluate and interpret it.

The concerns that my students arrive with, their desire to make friends and to be a part of a community that extended from family to school, have been for me a somewhat separate area of preschool life. I have tended to think of print with the approach described earlier, as something literal, as a problem to be solved. I see print as a tool. You uncover its functioning by logical analysis—and then you can make use of it to get at the richness of stories. The children in my class learned a good deal about print in this mode. But they also used the shadow curriculum to learn about print for other purposes. The children brought to me a sense of print as an avenue into these representations and interpretations of the world. I think that from their curriculum came the pleasure and the solemnity with which they set out to learn about the formal nature of print. If they had to approach this learning with my sense of its importance alone, as a tool, something to be analyzed, I don't believe they would have brought so much of themselves to bear on it; I don't believe they would have progressed so well.

I began with the thought that they were lacking in experience, experience we would have to make up for—and, of course, there was truth to that. But they didn't come with a lack of experience in general. They came with tasks that needed doing, and ideas about how they might accomplish them. I think that because I was able to "see" some of what they used print for, I was able to honor and respond to their intentions. In this way, many other children became engaged and the commitment of all to this area of learning was increased. This view powerfully enlarged what I considered relevant to learning about print in my classroom.

Would other children have developed the shadow curriculum, other children who are not Haitian? It has been a commonplace in the progressive, big-city classrooms where I have taught to note that the social is not antithetical to the intellectual in school learning. Nor do I doubt that for many children the goal is essentially to have friends. But I had not been truly clear on what we mean by this rather obvious statement. Are we talking about discussion, or about cooperative learning? In what sense is being friends part of learning to read or to count?

Documenting the experience of this group of engaged children and exploring their goals and mine has opened up for me a view of contact and interaction between social and intellectual goals in school in a way that neither trivializes the intentions of children nor the complexity of what they have to learn.

Chapter 6

STORYBOOK READING

When we read a storybook to young children, we talk about the book with them frequently, sometimes after the book is finished, sometimes during the story. Storybook reading includes not only the written text in the book, but the talk that goes on around the book. This talk is for the purpose of connecting with the book, of understanding it and its relation to our lives.

We have expectations about how this talk should go. Cochran-Smith (1985) in *The Making of a Reader* explains the kind of talk I would have expected at story time; she characterizes the talk that teachers value in these situations as talk that exemplifies a sort of mental movement from life to text for the purposes of better understanding the text. Teachers often help this to happen by the questions they ask, the "Do you have a doggie at your house?" sort of question, when a book about dogs is being read. The reader is helped to make sense of the book by connecting his or her own relevant experience to the book's topic. We want the children to move from their life experience to the text.

In this chapter and the next I will recount what are in my opinion the most complex and challenging experiences discussed in this book. These chapters are about stories and storybook reading. They contain many voices, and in this case, unfinished conversations, conversations that remain in some tension. As I read stories to my students, and thought about them, I could hear the voices of my mother and my friends, who regard storybook reading as private moments when we pass on a love of literature to children. I could hear as well the voices of Lisa Delpit and Courtney Cazden, who emphasize, among other things, that learning the rules is part of talking about literature or any discipline, and the voices of my young Haitian students, who never stopped talking about the books they loved. Never. I listened carefully to my Haitian colleagues as they told me stories and told me about storytelling in Haiti. And I listened to my colleagues at the BTRS who wanted to know precisely what the children were doing when we read stories, and precisely what I wanted them to be doing.

As a teacher and a researcher I knew well that children who are read to frequently at home are more likely to do well at school. As a parent I recognized myself in Heath's accounts of middle-class behavior. Reading books to my own children was an intimate time, and one that, when my children began to speak freely of books in relation to outside events—my

9-year-old son once quoting Dylan Thomas's phrase "snow-blind travelers" as we stepped out into a snowstorm—was a source of satisfaction. As a teacher, I felt the needs of these children, who had not had these experiences, who came from a culture where storybook reading was not a common part of family tradition. And so I entered this classroom with a strong sense of responsibility in this area—and what I thought was a strong record. Storybook reading was the heart of what I knew how to do with young children, and the heart of what I valued.

I began to share my favorite books with the children. They loved them, but, as they responded with their enthusiasm, I felt at sea. Their ways of responding to the books were unfamiliar, seemed wrong. As an American teacher in a classroom of Haitian children, I found myself engaged in many interactions with books that I found unfamiliar and quite disconcerting. I set out to discover what it was that seemed strange and unfamiliar. As I began to describe some of the ways the children in my classroom became involved with books, I realized that the children's responses to the books challenged long-buried assumptions of my own. I came to rethink some of my assumptions about the role of books in the classroom, in conversation, and in the larger world. These two chapters are the story of this process. However, they remain problematic for me because, I think, the uses of literature in the world are themselves so complex and vast, and the ways in which we connect imaginatively with it remain mysterious.

This chapter has two parts. I will begin with the concrete—the treatment of books, the recognition of them as particular kinds of objects. In the second part, I will talk about the ways in which we read books together. I place these together because I think that together they offer the fullest sense of how the children were engaging with this important area of schooling.

BOOKS AND CATALOGS

Among the assumptions teachers make as they begin early literacy experience with a class of children is that they share with the children at least a basic idea of what a book is and why we value it. When children begin to love books and to spend time with them, we further assume that they are beginning to know books in the way we know them. Here I will discuss the differences I discovered between my conception of a book and that of the children in my class.

When I took over my class of 3- to 6-year-olds in September I brought with me many of my favorite children's books. I put them in a display book case so that the children had ready access to them. In another area of the room I arranged art materials, crayons, paste, scissors, markers, paper, and old advertising catalogs from which they could cut pictures. Soon I began finding the catalogs out of the art area and with the books in the bookcase, put there by the children. More disturbing, the children were occasionally discovered cutting books as well as catalogs in the art corner.

I was not unduly upset. I knew that the children had few books at home, and in fact in this school before my arrival they usually had books only under strict supervision. The teacher might read to the children, but the children were not allowed to handle the books freely. The children had had few opportunities to learn about books, but I would change that, I thought. I saw it as a matter of categorization. This belongs here; that belongs there. These are the rules for books; these are the rules for catalogs. I set out to teach the distinction.

However, over time I was surprised at how intractable their confusion was. It seemed that we only succeeded in getting to the point where they would ask me before cutting something, but not to the point where they knew which was which.

In addition, I created a quiet corner for reading. However many times I arranged this, it never lasted long. Nobody wanted to be alone in it. They brought toys and friends, trucks and dolls, in there and read, both catalogs and books, as part of their play. Soon even I would lose track of the idea that this was supposed to be a place for someone to be alone.

Occasionally a child would come to school with a book. We would usually read the book and I would pay some attention to its whereabouts during the course of the day so that he could take it home in the afternoon. One afternoon as Jean's father was picking him up, it became clear that they were missing something. Jean and his father were searching the school. I vaguely remembered that Jean had arrived with a catalog, but I had paid no attention. I didn't know what had happened to it, but I began to help them search. Then Jean began to cry. I realize now that, when Jean began to cry, I saw his loss anew—this time not as a catalog, but as a book, and began looking for that instead. When the catalog was found and Jean stopped crying, I was astonished. How could he have been crying over a catalog?

Books have stories in them. Books arouse feelings and tap the imagination. What does a catalog have to do with stories or the imagination? Consider the following transcript of Eveline and Kenthea, engaged in one of their favorite activities: looking through a Sears catalog. They point at various items as they speak:

Example 1

Eveline: That's for me. That bed you can sleep in when you sleep over my house.
Kenthea: And that one is mine in my new house.

Eveline: That's me and those shoes are for me, and those.
Kenthea: We're sisters, OK, and we have those shoes.

To Kenthea and Eveline the catalog contains the most important story, the story of their friendship. The reading is contained in their interaction, very much as it is in the following, when Kenthea and Giles look at Bert and Ernie in a Sesame Street book in which Ernie and Bert are on a see-saw:

Example 2

Kenthea: I'm Ernie.
Giles: I'm Bert.
Kenthea: I'm up and you're down.

Kenthea and Giles use the pictures and their friendship to "read" this book. When Giles and Pierre look at a book whose plot they know, *Jack and the Beanstalk*, their relationship and the plot interact to structure their reading. In this dialogue, they begin talking to each other, but Pierre's final comment is made to me:

Example 3

Pierre: I'm the giant.
Giles: I'm Jack.
Pierre: I'm gonna eat Giles. [Smiling, somewhat surprised, he looks up at me.]

It doesn't matter if you have a catalog or a book if the story is about your relationship. The plot of this story will of course vary depending on the contribution of the text. In examples 1 and 2 the children insert their plot into the book and the catalog by using the pictures. In example 3 they put themselves as actors into the book's plot. The origin of the plot varies but the "reading" in all cases is a part of the relationship of the children. And yet I have told them, "No, you mustn't cut the books, they have stories in them. Cut the catalogs," I have said. "They have no stories."

There are different senses of things here, different ways of being involved with books, that I was, somewhat unconsciously, determined to teach. First, consider cutting, or in any way physically altering a book. To the children it seems reasonable to cut out things that they like. They carry them around. They mean no violence. I let them choose things that they like from catalogs to cut out, but not from books. To me, however, cutting a book is doing violence to the book, even if the particular picture is preserved intact. Cutting a book is doing violence even if I don't need that book. I would not cut a picture out of, say, a college astronomy textbook of mine, a book I will probably never open again, a book full of information that is undoubtedly now considerably out-of-date. I would certainly give this book away, and, with some difficulty, I might even throw it away, but I would not deface it or cut it. My copy of Proust, on the other hand, I don't think I could throw away, certainly not in the trash. I disliked it and never finished it, and, of course, there are multiple copies in the local library, but to get rid of it I would have to give it to a second-hand book store, where there is the illusion that someone else might buy it and read it. I would never cut a children's book, even if I had multiple copies. I understand easily when a friend of mine tells me of his distress when a book he had loaned was returned with passages underlined; the borrower, a student of his, had evidently underlined what he considered important. The book, of course, remained entirely legible, and yet my friend was very disturbed at what had been done, to him somehow, as well as to the book. He, since he has a large library, tells the IRS each year on his tax return how much less his books are worth than the previous year—and yet he can part with these increasingly worthless objects only with enormous difficulty.

Books are precious, something I treat with care, something I separate from other toys, other paper, other text. These patterns of behavior and emotion are finally rather difficult to explain. My behavior, the behavior of many of us, in an age of printing and photocopying, suggests that we might truly be adherents of a cult in which books have sacred value, value beyond what can be explained by common sense.

John Willinsky (1990) is perhaps attempting to describe this cult when he suggests that for many educated people, reading great literature is seen as the source through which they truly become themselves as unique individuals. "Literature might well be thought of as a font for anointing our individuality," he claims (p. 215). When my son asks me if we have a copy of Thoreau's *Walden* I tell him I am sure we do, although I don't immediately know where. He asks me why we keep it, since I am clearly not very involved with it anymore, and I have a sense of seeing my own picture almost, at the age of 16 or 17, the age he is as he asks, in that book. On further reflection I realize that there are many books I keep because I feel they are like time-lapse photographs of myself at various points of becoming who I am. This idea sounds somewhat narcissistic but I think, in fact, narcissistic or not, it is rather widely held. I know I am not alone in this because I look in the bookcases of friends and see many of the same sort of things there, books they will probably never read again but that appear to be serving as a reminder of something quite important. I think it is this that Willinsky is trying to identify when he says "a font of our individuality"; we, my friends and I, regard certain books as embodying some of our values and our outlook on life, as marking a spot where these were acquired or articulated. They are consequently quite important to our understanding of who we are.

With such an attitude toward books, no wonder I lose my patience as the children cut or color in the classroom books, as they read them in the middle of truck play, as they sit on them to keep the monsters in. And yet for these children, as we have seen in the above texts, books are not significantly different from catalogs, nor is an area without trucks crashing and dolls crying a place to be preferred in order to "read" them. The children saw books as something to enjoy in the same way that they enjoyed the other things they were given at school, that is, with their friends. For the children, books belonged in a context of friends and play; for me books belonged in an intensely private context of peace and quiet.

STORYBOOK READING

Let me now turn to a different kind of relationship with books: storybook reading, my favorite time of day. The children loved it too. But I found both what they said and did while I was reading very unfamiliar. My field notes from the first three months of the school year document my frustration.

10/5
   Reading books seems to be an invitation to a conversation. All I could hear was Cindy, Cindy, Cindy.

10/12
   Tried to read *3 Bears*. Nobody listened.

11/7
   Story reading to J's group. The children were delighted. They jumped into the book in the sense that Jérémie chose who he would play with in the snow house pictured. Rubenson said he wanted to bring a carpet into the snow house pictured in the book. When the snowman is pictured all the children jump up to show how big they would make theirs. Picture of one kid hitting another with a snow-ball—Rubenson tries to act it out. Hits Jérémie.

11/8
   Read *Are You My Mother?* to Emmanuel. When Emmanuel is asking "Where's the mother?" someone from Play-doh™ table replies that he'll make one for him.

11/14
Reading was awful again. Kids won't listen to me. All talk at
once. Still they seem happy and engaged during reading—but why?

11/15
Circle was bearable. Did very peaceful songs. Read *Dinnertime*, a
pop-up book where one animal eats the next. The first book this
group as a group has sat through. They jumped up and down, and
they talked, but we almost finished the book in one session.

11/30
We only live with two books so far: *Are You My Mother?* and
Dinnertime.

12/6
Read *3 Bears* today. Read while they were at lunch—I thought
maybe they would be quieter that way. They weren't. Found myself
teaching rules of storybook reading: "It's nice for you to be quiet
when I am telling a story"; "You need to sit when we read stories,
it's one of the rules." Almost all of my comments outside of actual
reading were about rules this time. Still I was able to ask why the
baby bear was crying and Emmanuel knew—"paske li kraze chèz li
a. Li renmen chèz li" (because she broke his chair. He loves his
chair). And Kenthea too, "because him broke him's chair."

Three months into the year and it still seemed to me that books had not
taken hold. The children were too noisy, they were always calling out,
always commenting, always jumping up to punch the monsters in the book
or to act it out. They were not listening. What they were doing was not, in
my opinion, a part of book reading. I dreaded it. And yet they seemed to
enjoy it.

The Paradox

However, as I complained, I nevertheless had to admit that books were
becoming an important part of a very lively classroom. Again let me give
the flavor by the following:

11/10
There are 8 children in the classroom today. 7 of them are playing together as a family. Leslie, just 3 years old and the youngest of
the lot, is the mother, and carries a doll around. Everyone else is
somehow related, grandmother, sister, cousins, brothers. Leslie states

that the baby is sick. They scurry off from one side of the room to the other, evidently searching for help for the baby. As they confer, with their faces to the wall, Eveline, who has been excluded, begins lining up chairs two-by-two. She completes four pairs and puts one chair in the front. The children, still buzzing about the sick baby, turn around. As they see what Eveline has done, their faces shine. Obviously this is a bus to take them to the hospital. They dash for their seats. Eveline is accepted as the driver. Then Leslie remembers—"we forgot the books," and rushes off to the book case. There she takes a book for every child (by some luck since she does not bother to count and in fact does not fully understand the relation between counting and quantity) and one for the baby. The children take their seats on the bus, open their books, and go off to the hospital. Once there, with their books now under their arms, they try to get help. Although they give it medicine, the baby dies anyway. Fortunately, it soon comes back to life.

Books here figure in a life-and-death situation—they are obviously very important.

It is a few weeks later that I begin to have a vague but increasing awareness that books are disappearing from the classroom, and then reappearing some time later without any effort on my part. Finally, by chance, I discover that Emmanuel is keeping them in his bag.

12/5

Emmanuel seems to see the different activities in the classroom as part of a larger drama he is enacting. He spends the morning going from activity to activity with a big, old, woman's pocketbook, which he calls his "valise," over his shoulder. He takes it outside on the playground with him. He hangs it up carefully next to the water table before he rolls up his sleeves to play there. He has devised many complex ways to attach it to the different riding toys available. Nobody would think of taking it from him. In it he places various treasures, drawings, letter stencils, circulars that are among the art table materials, pens, and, as it turns out, books. Although I knew he was often looking at books, I hadn't seen him taking the books out of the valise and so I didn't realize he was keeping them there.

Evidently I had some expectation that art materials, since they are to be worked on and then taken home, were reasonable things to carry around in one's personal bag, but books were public property and I did not expect to find them there. To Emmanuel, however, these were all part of the life he was leading in his imagination as he drove on his big wheel around the classroom.

This final field note contains another aspect of the children's engagement with books:

> 12/5
>
> All the children seemed to me to need instruction on caring for books. They would read them on the rug, leave them there, and then later walk all over them without a thought. I explained insistently about not stepping on the books any number of times. A few days later I found Kenthea with six books, all laid out in a large rectangle on the floor. She appeared to be prancing around them. When I ask her what she is doing, she tells me, "I'm not stepping on the books."
>
> She has perhaps not entirely got the point, for a few days later she asked me for the monster book. I gave her *Jack and the Beanstalk*, and she proceeded to sit on it with evident solemnity. I was at a loss—so again I asked, what are you doing with the book? "I don't want no monster get out," she told me.

I began to recognize that, although we may not easily finish books, and story reading may not be an intimate and meditative time, books are a part of the life of the classroom. It was becoming clear that they loved them and regarded them as powerful. Their kindergarten teachers would appreciate that—perhaps some part of my job *was* getting done. And yet an unsettling tension remained between the way I wanted them to respond to books and the way they wanted to. I was excited by what I saw them doing—and yet nervous about what was missing.

Approach to the Task

In discussion with the BTRS, a number of questions emerged at this point. What made me think that the children were cheerful and engaged, but not appropriately so? What could I mean by that? What exactly were they doing wrong? And why? What is the goal of book reading anyway? As stated earlier, in the BTRS we often find ourselves focusing on aspects of our own values in relation to both practice and research (see Chapters 4 & 5). We have come to see that investigating, interpreting, and identifying what the children are doing in a particular area is a way for the teacher to delve into the area himself or herself in order to learn what it is and what it really means, for the teacher as well as for the children. It is not something that I think I finished in this case, but it is this sort of wide net that I tried to cast in exploring their book reading and my own.

Let me begin by trying to articulate more completely what I found in my attitude toward storybook reading as a teacher; I will then turn to an exploration of what the children were doing with books. In my classroom I had always made storybook reading one of the central events of the day; in fact, I had often thought that it was the only really crucial event in a preschool day—anything else that seemed important, for example, number concepts or information about nature, could be made to flow from the story reading. Stories to a large extent were the curriculum. I have come to realize that book reading is also the core of a particular relationship I enjoy, or have enjoyed in the classrooms of the last 15 years, with the children. I read dramatically and encourage response—I expect the children to "bring themselves" to the reading, to participate. I do not insist on silence at all; however, I also expect the children to be engrossed. Storybook reading is a time of some emotional intensity. Some children do not respond verbally; others may perhaps respond by telling me a personal story, by asking a question, or making a comment, but they are ideally engaged in what Bruner (quoting Jorge Luis Borges) calls "guided dreaming" (Bruner, 1984). Guided dreaming seems to capture the sense of intense and yet meditative engagement that characterizes, in my understanding, this activity. Although it is a group activity, there is something very private about it. For example, I think I particularly value a child who is so "engrossed" as we read as to be almost oblivious to the other children. I think this is what reading was for me as a child—a valued time alone to be "myself." I don't think I am unusual in this—it is probably for this reason that so many teachers and parents use storybook reading as a way to calm children down before sleeping or naps.

Some aspect of the problem was becoming clear. I realized now that the children were violating a sense I had of what our relationship in this context ought to be. They were supposed to be meditative, entranced. We were supposed to feel very close and to be sharing a quiet moment altogether. No wonder I was upset.

Texts: Their Book Reading

I decided to look closely at some sessions of book reading in order to determine more clearly what their approach was. I chose the following session for detailed investigation because it seemed to embody the paradox I was living with, which was that, although it felt quite chaotic to me, the children seemed at the same time very intense and engaged. The book that we read at this session, *Dinnertime*, became a part of the classroom culture—the children referred to it in conversations among themselves and with me; they often carried it with them as they went through the day; they requested it very frequently, and they would read it to themselves as well as with me. And yet, as I said, what they had to say did not feel familiar to me and did not seem "right."

The following is from the first reading session of *Dinnertime*, a storybook by Jan Pienkowski. In this book a series of animals appear one after the other, each new one eating the last. This is the first time the children sat through any book reading as a group. Although individuals had read stories with me before this day, the entire group had not.

The reading and the children's responses alternate between Haitian Creole (HC) and English. I have included the language as it was spoken, with translation in parentheses. Italics indicate the words that are from the book.

1. *Jérémie*: Cindy, what is this? [pointing at picture in book]
2. *Cindy*: It's a book, oh, I think it's a shark. [I spend a moment organizing seating so that all can see]
3. *Cindy*: *One day a frog . . .*
4. *Jérémie*: He got mouth?
5. *Cindy*: *One day a frog was sitting on a log catching flies when down came a vulture.*
6. *Jérémie*: Cindy he got mouth.
7. *Cindy*: Yes, they all have mouths. *Vulture said to frog "I'm going to eat you for my dinner"* [pointing to vulture] m pral manje ou (I'm gonna eat you) *and that's what he did.*
8. *Jérémie*: Li di li pral manje moun? (he said he will eat people?)
9. *Cindy*: Non, li mèm, li di "m pral manje ou" (no, that one he said, "I will eat you").
10. *Jérémie*: Manje on frog (eat a frog)?
11. *Cindy*: Yeah li pral manje on frog (he will eat a frog).

We go on in similar fashion, identifying who will eat whom, until in line 39 Jérémie begins to enter into the story.

39. *Jérémie*: M pral pran on kouto pou m ka koupe li (I will get a knife so I can cut him).
40. *Cindy*: Ou pral koupe li? (You will cut him?)
41. *Rubenson*: Yes, li mèm (yes, that one).
42. *Jérémie*: Li gen de dan (he has two teeth) [showing two fingers in each hand].
43. *Cindy*: De? pa kat? ah wi, de anba, de anwo, sa fè konbyen? un, de, twa, kat (two? not four? oh yes, two below, two above, that makes how many? 1,2,3,4).
44. *Jérémie*: M pral manje li mèm (I will eat that one).

45. *Rubenson*: Li pral mouri (he's gonna die).
46. *Cindy*: Li mèm? sa k fè ou konnen (him? how do you know)?
47. *Rubenson*: [no response]
48. *Cindy*: Poukisa li pral mouri (why is he gonna die)?
49. *Rubenson*: Li pral koupe li (he's gonna cut him).
50. *Jérémie*: Li mèm, m pa renmen li (I don't like that one).

I question the boys because I am assuming that, after counting the teeth, they have returned to the text and are drawing inferences from it. Thus when Rubenson says "He will die," referring to the animal on the page—a shark—I assume he is making a prediction based on the story structure—a reasonable prediction since that is exactly what has happened to each new animal in turn. I ask him to explain how he knows, since this sort of basis for prediction is what I am used to bringing out in storybooks. In fact, as Rubenson tells me, he is not making a prediction from the text—he is instead referring to Jérémie's statement that Jérémie will cut the shark. Jérémie then helpfully explains to me why he will cut him: because he doesn't like him. When they act like this, they appear to me to be acting inside the story itself. I came to call it "entering-in." They enter into the text and change it at will. I expect them to imagine themselves in the book, and perhaps to explore and comment on this experience, but I don't think they should change what the text said.

Below the two boys continue this sort of interaction by describing what will happen between them and the animals, and then enacting the fight they have predicted.

52. *Rubenson*: Li pral tonbe (he will fall).
53. *Kids*: [Unintelligible talk, excited by Rubenson and Jérémie's story].
54. *Cindy*: [to others] Stop talking. Kote li pral tonbe (Where will he fall)?
55. *Rubenson*: Li pral tonbe atè a (he will fall on the ground).
56. *Rubenson*: Lèfini li pral tonbe atè a (and then he will fall on the ground).
57. *Rubenson*: Lèfini M al bat li atè a (and then I will beat him on the ground).
[Enacts whole fight with further commentary]

When I ask, "Where will he fall?" (line 54), I have reassumed my unshakeable conviction that statements of this sort are inferences made from the text. And I am wrong again. Rubenson is instead diverging from the text in order to include his own actions in the story.

Below, Jérémie builds in his turn on Rubenson's scenario to explain once more why he does not like that animal.

58. *Jérémie*: M pa renmen li mèm (I don't like that one)
59. *Jérémie*: Paske li mèm ki pral manje m (because it's he who will eat me).
60. Rubenson di li pral pran on [unintelligible] pou bat li (Rubenson said he will take a [?] to beat him).
61. Li pral monte sou do m (he will get on my back).
62. Li pral mode m (he'll bite me).

Jérémie was excited; he appeared to me to be actually somewhat frightened, as he explained to me what he feared the animal would do to him and what Rubenson would do.

I next manage to read a few lines of the text before Jérémie, and then Pierre, "enter in" again (lines 80 and 85).

68. *Cindy*: *Tiger bounded into the water to wash his whiskers and there was a crocodile.*
69. *Kids:* Cindy Cindy.
70. *Pierre*: Crocodile.
71. *Cindy*: Crocodile *crocodile said, I'm going to eat you for my dinner.*
72. *Jérémie*: Ki moun (who)?
73. *Cindy*: He's gonna eat him.
74. *Jérémie*: Tiger?
75. *Cindy*: Yes, crocodile's gonna eat tiger *and he did. Crocodile wiped his eyes and floated lazily out to sea and there he met a shark.*
76. *Jérémie*: Fish!!
77. *Cindy*: Big, gwo (big) fish. It's called a shark.
78. *Jérémie*: M al cheche on kouto (I will go find a knife).
79. [Enacts fight]
80. *Jérémie*: M al chire/touye (??) (I'll I'll tear/kill).
81. *Cindy*: All right, all right.
82. *Kenthea*: You see, you see, Cindy, that fish do that like this [commenting on how shark swims].
83. *Cindy*: Yeah, he can swim like that.
84. *Pierre*: Cindy, m al retire gwo dan li (I will take out his big teeth).
85. *Cindy*: Ou pral retire gwo dan li (you will take out his big teeth)?
86. *Jérémie*: No, me! [DISPUTING]
87. *Jérémie*: M al, m al, m al (I'll I'll, I'll).
88. *Cindy*: You wanna see what the book says happens? Let's see what the book says.
89. *Jérémie*: No.

Pierre's offering, "I will take out his big teeth," is disputed by Jérémie, who says he will do it instead. When I suggest we should find out what the book says about all of this, Jérémie disagrees.

My Problems

Who Gets to Talk. My first problem was the sheer amount of participation, the volume of what they had to say. Like many of us, I would claim that, both as a teacher and as a parent, I believed strongly that storybook reading was an interactive process in which teachers and children together arrive at the meaning. Even though their questions and their comments indicated to me that they were engaged, I felt that I was being battered with something I thought I relished. I could not imagine telling children to be quiet in this context but it felt to me like they had too much to say.

There are many articles in which researchers have transcribed teachers reading with children or mothers reading with children, and in going through these I discovered that what I typically practiced may have been less interactive than I supposed. In these transcriptions, conversational exchanges initiated by children around storybooks are rare to nonexistent, both in mainstream homes and at school. In storybook reading in preschool the conversation appears entirely one-sided (Cochran-Smith, 1985; Dickinson & Keebler, 1989). Teachers initiate most, and sometimes all, of the interaction in the data presented in these articles. Children may talk but they mainly respond to the adult. The few times when a child initiates a comment that is acknowledged, rather than ignored, by the teacher, it is generally followed by a direct question by means of which the teacher takes back direction of the conversation. As an example, consider the following typical talk around books included in *The Making of a Reader*. The teacher is reading to the children a book about fossils when a child tries to bring up a gerbil:

Teacher: That fish became a fossil.
Child: . . . And when his gerbil died, he took it to the garbage.
Teacher: And did he bury it somewhere?
Child: He— (several children still talking)
Teacher: Is it gonna turn into a rock and become a fossil, do you do you think? Be mashed into rock—
Child: Yeah (uncertainly). (Cochran-Smith, 1985, p. 195)

Here a child has a topic, which the teacher acknowledges, and then immediately begins asking questions in order to lead the child back to the book's topic, in this case, fossils. The book's topic is considered primary, and children are helped to make their remarks relevant to it. In the accounts of mothers reading to their children (for example, Snow & Ninio, 1986; Taylor, 1986), the level of child initiation is higher, but the conversation is still clearly in the control of the mother, and as Snow and Ninio point out, in storybook reading in the middle-class home, "if the child's topic cannot be made relevant . . . , the mother either prohibits it or terminates the book reading session" (p. 125).

My students, in contrast, talked an enormous amount and initiated many topics. They talked often to me, but also to each other, and they carried on with their topics. The book was one voice among many, it seemed, not central.

My students had not had the experience of reading storybooks with their parents. They had not been guided to see the book as a controlling topic, one to which everything must be made relevant. I, as the representative of the book, was accustomed to being in control of this conversation, but I had never really been aware of having to control it in the past. It had just seemed to happen. Lacking certain experience in their homes, they nevertheless came to the book with ideas of how to participate. I expected them to "dream" the story as I read it to them; they instead participated so fully with the book's characters that they were likely to take over the story line.

I was worried about their comprehension of the book. Why wouldn't they follow the story as written? Let me first consider this question in regard to *Dinnertime* and then return to it in the next chapter.

Whose View of the World? First, there is the question of genre. *Dinnertime*, while giving an account of a violent sequence of one animal eating another, has a somewhat comical tone to my ears. These children did not appear to find it comical, however. They acted horrified by it, perhaps a little shocked that I would read it to them. Haitian children are not familiar with stories about cute or cuddly animals the way many American children are. Nor do they have much tolerance for stories that condone bad behavior, however it is presented. My students disliked *The Runaway Bunny* for example, which is typically seen as a nurturing book about a bunny who continually runs away and his mother who is always there for him; one of my students exclaimed in horror when I read that one, "My mother would kill me if I did that." They were alarmed by Curious George's behavior in some cases as well.

Stories like *Dinnertime* or *Little Red Riding Hood*, in which one character eats another, were generally regarded as truly scary, and as containing lessons that ought to be followed by children wishing to avoid this fate. My students were a moral lot and took proper behavior seriously. *Dinnertime* was perhaps particularly disconcerting in that there was not a moral. They seemed unsettled by it.

Imagining a Story? And yet, as unsettled as they were, their imaginations were going full tilt. Their responses were full of detail. They truly imagined themselves there: "He will get on my back. He will bite me." They often told me similar stories without the aid of a book: "I was out with my family, and I jumped in the water, and a shark came, and he took me, and my father jumped in, and he punched that shark and he pulled me out" (Pierre, 4 years old). They were concerned about these hungry animals and were engaging with this story on their own terms.

Their chatter around *Dinnertime*, when I heard it on tape, reminded me of what I heard when they were playing in the house corner. I realized that my students were in a sense playing *in* the story I was reading. I began to think about the value of this kind of play. In the house corner it seems to me that children are able to explore roles, for example, that of father and baby, or neighbor, police officer, whatever they have included; they argue over their understandings of these roles and develop plots that test what they think they know. They connect with roles, with how characters might feel, and with the feeling of imagining different lives, different realities. Was this what they were doing with *Dinnertime*? In the unfamiliar genre, where animal after animal gets eaten and no moral is drawn, they were perhaps trying to develop a story they could relate to. They were injecting some passion, some conflict, some emotions into it as they added their own episodes.

How do we become involved with a book, particularly if it is somewhat foreign? How do we enter into any fictional world? I had never asked. There had been, in my experience, stories I had been unable to appreciate. I had never been able to enjoy the Coyote trickster stories that are a part of the traditions of some Native-American groups or the Bouki and Malice stories from the Haitian tradition, which are somewhat similar. They just didn't seem interesting or compelling to me although I knew they were to other people. Then one day I heard an old Haitian grandmother tell some Bouki and Malice stories. She acted out all the parts, used sound effects and different voices, and I loved them. I've been able to enjoy reading them ever since. I understood something that I hadn't understood before, how the stories are enjoyed, by watching the grandmother play in them. Perhaps, by imagining themselves in the story, by acting within it like the storyteller I heard, like they play in the house corner, the children were experiencing the story in some way they otherwise couldn't.

Recall their earlier interactions with books and catalogs. There again they inserted themselves inside, owning the shoes in the catalog, putting their relationships into the books. I was reminded of Paley's (1990) account of storytelling in her nursery school classroom. There too the children created stories and "entered in" to them. Paley sees the value of this approach to literature: "Stories that are not acted out are fleeting dreams: private fantasies, disconnected and unexamined" (p. 25).

How do we imagine ourselves into a book? How do we empathize with characters and situations? What are the range of ways? And how does the story as told figure in this imaginative act? Does anyone do it exactly as written? In the next chapter, these questions are developed further.

Chapter 7

"NOW THE ROBBERS IS NICE"

In their conversations around *Dinnertime*, the children demonstrated some of their ways of participating in this talk around storybooks, ways that I was not accustomed to. The next book we read together was *The Three Robbers* by Tomi Ungerer. From the first day we read it, they talked about it, discussed it, carried it around with them during the school day. It was important to them. Yet it was a long time before we ever managed to finish it. They had too much to say; the discussion would go far afield and I would have to put the book down. Their comments didn't seem to me to be relevant to the book. I felt that they had too much to say as we read and that it wasn't on topic.

When we did finish the book, I had additional concerns: They refused to believe the story as written. In the story the three robbers spend their time robbing stagecoaches; they use a pepper-blower to blow pepper in the horses' eyes, a blunderbuss to scare the passengers, and an axe to chop up the stagecoaches' wheels. However, one night it happens that there are no rich passengers to plunder. The only one in the coach is an orphan named Tiffany who is going to live with a wicked aunt. So the robbers take her back to their cave and put her cozily to bed. The next morning when she wakes up she sees all their treasure. She asks them, "What is all this for?" The robbers had never thought of this; they had never realized there might be a purpose for all their wealth. At this point, they decide to set up a home for all the lost and abandoned children in the world and they become "kind foster fathers." My students did not accept that the robbers had become good. My authority was not sufficient. Their view seemed to be that no book would say such a thing or should. How we developed a shared understanding of *The Three Robbers* is what I will recount here. As will be apparent, it was not a straight road.

The following transcript is from the very first time we read *The Three Robbers*.

Leslie: This is the 3 robbers?
Eveline: 3 robbers, I'm 3, I'm 3, I'm 3.
Cindy: Yeah, 1,2,3. Be quiet, sit down. If you wanta hear, don't talk,
   OK? It says the three robbers [pointing at title] *Once upon a time*

there were three fierce robbers. They went about hidden under large black capes and tall black hats.

Eveline: Lemme see.

Cindy: If you wanta see, come sit.

Jean: One eye [unintelligible] only one.

Cindy: Yeah, it looks like he's only got one eye he's got his hat down here.

Jean: Only two eyes [evidently referring to himself].

Cindy: Yeah, I think this guy has probably got two eyes but his hat is down. You know he's hiding so nobody knows who he is cuz he's bad.

Jean: Why?

Jean-Marc: Bad guy!!!

Cindy: *The first had a blunderbuss* you see this kind of a gun—

Jean: Gun gun.

Cindy: It's called a blunderbuss, it's kind of a gun.

Jean: Yeah.

Cindy: *The second had a pepper-blower.* You see that? It puts piman in people's eyes, you see that, pepper.

Jean: Pepper?

Cindy: Yeah, pepper, it's piman.

Giles: My daddy eat piman . . . I eat piman.

Cindy: You eat piman too?

Leslie: My daddy eat piman.

Jean: Everybody eat piman.

Leslie: [unintelligible] food.

Cindy: Do you like it in your eyes?

Kids: [unintelligible] daddy piman I like it . . . .

Cindy: But in your eyes?

Jean: No. No eyes.

Suzanne: I like it . . . my mother say . . . .

Leslie: Cindy, I eat in my eyes.

Kenthea: I drink my medicine myself. Cindy, I drink my medicine. My mother take medicine too.

Suzanne: My mother give me my medicine, green medicine.

TALK AROUND BOOKS—MY STUDENTS' VIEW

The children are initiating all the talk here and they are talking to each other; they're building on each others' remarks. They're having a wonderful time. To me, however, they seem to be ignoring the book. I try to bring their attention back to it. I find myself, in this case and in others like it, frustratedly holding up the book to the children's view as if I thought they had forgotten it, or me.

Should I shut this engagement down? I brought this problem to the BTRS, and they wanted to know what the children were talking about. What did their enthusiastic response contain? Since I had this conversation on tape, I was able to listen to it at a calmer moment, after school. In this more reflective mode, I recognized more than one of the children's seemingly random remarks from other moments in the school day. Eveline responds to the word three in the title, *The Three Robbers*: "I'm 3, I'm 3, I'm 3." She has a very positive feeling about it because she associates it closely with herself. She will fight anyone who believes that he or she is also 3. She greets the number, not by exploring its role in the text, but by saying something important about herself with it.

Jean contrasts his situation to the robber's—the robber only has one eye (or so it appears from the picture) while Jean has two. In fact Jean's reference to eyes is a recurring theme in his play and conversation. A few days before we read *The Three Robbers* he had told a story about throwing sugar in a dog's eyes. His interest in eyes and maybe in the form of his body symmetry reapppears a few days later when he is finding a partner to walk outside with.

Jean: Cindy, hold my hand?
Cindy: I only have two hands, Jean [that is, both are already being held].
Jean: Two hands, two eyes, one mouth [with evident satisfaction].

Jean remains concerned with aspects of this issue throughout the year; the final appearance I note is in a version of *Jack and the Beanstalk* that he told near the end of the year.

> Once upon a time there was zombie
> Zombie no wanta eat Jack
> Jack want some food
> And big giant in the house
> Mother say no, big giant in the house
> And big zombie
> Jack have a rock
> Jack throw the rock in the zombie's eyes
> And zombie's eye get out
> Only one eye stay

Eveline and Jean have moved away from the central meaning of the text; neither eyes nor the number three is a main theme of *The Three Robbers*.

They do not appear to be moving from their experience back to the text, as Cochran-Smith (1985) suggests they should. And yet, even though they presumably already knew their age and the number of their eyes, one senses a great force behind their statements. These are the sorts of comments that teachers of young children puzzle over all the time—statements of completely obvious facts, stated with enormous conviction and pride.

The discussion about piman/pepper has a similar feeling of engaged and excited public pronouncement. In the book, pepper is used by robbers to stop the stagecoach. But these children are talking about pepper in a different way. Piman is a central spice in Haitian cooking. An adult Haitian is expected to eat food with piman, hot food; for children, however, the piman is often left out. When I serve them unfamiliar food they often question me, "Pa gen piman?/it doesn't have piman?" to be sure before they are willing to taste it.

Again, they do not appear to be using their experience to move to an understanding of the book's meaning, but their enthusiasm suggests we should look more closely at what they are saying here. Giles introduces one theme, "My daddy eat piman." Leslie seconds this. Jean then makes the generalization, "Everybody eat piman." Leslie appears to be further specifying where piman is found. I then intervene by asking them to connect their discussion to the story line in typical teacher fashion, "Do you like it in your eyes?" I am concerned with their comprehending the book. This sort of remark, in many classrooms where I have taught, would bring the children right back to the book. Here, after Jean answers me, the children return and reprise, all together and therefore untranscribably, their knowledge of piman. From what I can understand of that segment, they are mentioning various people who eat piman and others who don't. Then Leslie says, "Cindy, I eat in my eyes" and laughs as she says this; I believe she was making a joke by joining my focus, "pepper in the eyes," with theirs, "eating." Finally, Kenthea brings up her ability, and her mother's, to take medicine by herself, a point Suzanne seconds.

The children are identifying the place of piman in their world and in their fathers' world. Piman is for adults. It is a sign of maturity. It is apparently particularly fathers who like the very hot food, so pepper is a sign of masculinity. Perhaps it is no coincidence that it is two girls, Kenthea and Suzanne, who make an analogy between taking medicine and eating piman. Mothers are associated with the power of medicine in a way similar to the father-piman connection. It is a sign of responsible adult status to be able to "eat piman" and to "drink my medicine myself." Both are difficult, but worth it. Through this highly interactive talk, the children have begun to interpret, for themselves and for me, the meaning of piman in their families and their culture.

Of course, maturity and adult status is a topic that occurs in other areas of the classroom as well. The piman discussion reminds me of a story told me by Leslie, the 3-year-old who, as the mother of the sick baby, handed out the books on the way to the hospital in the previous chapter. In this she too seems to be discussing the theme of maturity in terms of what you eat:

Cindy: What happened at your house yesterday?
Leslie: Nadine go to school
    Mommy go to work
    Daddy go to work
    I stay home by myself
    And I watch TV
    And I shower by myself
    Yesterday
Cindy: You did?
Leslie: I didn't cry in my house by myself.
Cindy: Oh, you didn't cry?
Leslie: Because I make Ovaltine by myself.

Leslie is not a good eater, and Ovaltine is her mother's way of making sure she gets important vitamins. Her mother makes sure she has it everyday, even bringing it into school to be finished if necessary. Here Leslie works with similar themes to those of medicine and piman in considering maturity and dependence. She takes on her mother's role with the Ovaltine, and so has the strength to be alone as well. These themes exist in the air of the classroom.

Throughout their discussion of *The Three Robbers*, the children are aware of the book in various ways, but they are focusing on issues situated in their world, not necessarily in the book. Their interpretation of the role of piman/pepper in Haitian culture is not a part of the story. The book is not the center of this conversation. In Cochran-Smith's (1985) terms, they are moving not from life to text, but the other way. Also, I am not the center. They are talking to each other. This conversation, like so many others I experienced this year, left me feeling sort of breathless. The children, on the other hand, seemed quite pleased with what they had done.

TALK AROUND BOOKS—MY COMMUNITY'S VIEW

I was concerned that my students and I had different views of book reading and what one ought to talk about at that time. And yet, as I said, the children were enormously serious. In wondering about this, I came to question my own assumptions about this talk and what it should contain. I decided to follow closely the conversations among my friends in which they discussed books. I wanted to know how such conversations were conducted outside of school.

I found that the practice of literate adults, even teachers, when they are talking about books outside of school is not the same as the practice of the same people in school. What I heard as I listened was more similar to the Haitian children's talk than I had expected. These conversations may begin with the book, but various topics arise as time goes on, not necessarily focusing on those elements that are necessary to literal comprehension of particular story lines. For example, I was recently part of a conversation about a book in which two of the characters were cousins; the conversation among the adults turned to recollection of various kinds of trouble participants had gotten into as children with cousins and then to speculations as to why cousins appear to get into more trouble together than nonrelations. This was not a central theme of the book. The goal of this adult discussion was not to comprehend the book, but rather to use the book to understand ourselves.

We, like the children in my class, act as if the information in the text were quite continuous with our lives. Thus we take from these books information and attitudes that speak to our larger concerns, to the conversations we are having with ourselves and with others on topics of importance to us. But is it a matter of ignoring the text's own meaning? Or is it rather that the process of fitting the book's story into one's own larger concerns is a part of comprehending and interpreting it? My now deeper understanding of the role of cousins in our lives, while not a central theme of that book, is thematically related and has become a part of the weave of the plot and character.

We certainly may attempt very carefully to follow the text, especially when the author is speaking directly to our topic, but in other cases we take events and characters from the book and use them in the arguments and ideas we are developing on our own topics, as the children did around piman or eyes. All of us, Haitian preschoolers and literate mainstream adults, read and talk that way all the time. It is almost as if reference to a book means "let's talk about important things."

But is that all we do? Will that ever lead to understanding the book as written? As I listened and thought about my own ways of reading, I realized that there are also instances when we don't wrest control from the book or make the book address our own concerns to the exclusion of its own. Sometimes we let the book take us places we haven't been, didn't even know about. In this case we read in order to incorporate the imagined experience of the novel into our own experiences, to make sense of people and events with the help of experiences we've gained from books, to learn about people we might not otherwise know. So a woman reads a memoir of the childhood of a very rich boy, and realizes something of the loneliness of her husband, whose background was similar. A novel that includes a very religious character helps a reader who lives a secular life to understand something of the character of religion.

Were my students using literature to imagine experiences they had not had and were unfamiliar with? Were they willing to let the book lead? And if so, did these experiences challenge them, expand their views? It would seem not, since they wouldn't believe me about what happened in the book, since they insisted on their own interpretations and ignored what the book had to say. Whether or not they spoke about issues important to them, and in ways analogous to those of literate adults, we still had to agree on the basic line of the plot. I was afraid we would never come to understand the book. How would they manage in kindergarten?

THE SOURCES OF INTERPRETATION

The robbers had become good and my students refused to believe it. Robbers are bad and they don't change, they said. I must be wrong about the book.

Did they think they could change what was written? I became convinced that they did think this. Consider Giles, for example. Giles has always been concerned about life and literature and the relation between them (see Chapter 5), but he is perhaps a little narrow in what he considers worthy themes for literature. He does not seem to accept stories unless the question of a mother and her possible death is a part of the plot. Here he proposes a way to make sure that this theme is included in *The Tortoise and the Hare*. I am almost at the end of the book when I close it in order to respond to a discussion about whether we have school the following day. Giles has been trying to get my attention:

Giles: Cindy, Cindy, lemme talk.
Cindy: OK, let's listen to Giles.
Giles: Open the book. [I open it up to our current page, a picture of the hare, which we are calling a rabbit.]
Giles: [looking at the picture intently] The rabbit mommy's dead the bad guy get a knife and he [unintelligible] another one rabbit get a knife [I start to close the book while listening to him] open the book

[I re-open the book]
and the bad guy rabbit [unintelligible]

This is only one of several times that Giles attempts to include in my reading a piece of plot involving the death of a mother. This time, however, he is particularly insistent that the book be open as he tells his part of the story, and as he does so, he stares fixedly at the book as if he were finding something in there. As you may remember (Chapter 5), Giles at the art table is continuously making happy and sad faces; he tells us they are his own face and the explanation for the sad face, when he is asked, is that his mother has died (which she has not in reality).

Like the others, he seems to find in literature a context for considering the themes that absorb him in the rest of his life. However, if the story does not speak to his concern, Giles is willing to insert it cleverly among the book's events. In this way, Giles is perhaps moving his life into the text, but not in the way Cochran-Smith (1985) intends.

How could I help them understand how text really worked? We read *The Three Robbers* over and over and I did tell them frequently that the robbers had become good. I would tell them that the book said so and point to the print. I felt bound to get across to them the authority of the text, which was what I thought was at issue. They, however, had gone to work to make sense of my insistence, as they understood it.

Ethics and Literature

I had noticed that all the children were interested in "bad" people. One book, in which a peripheral character is put in jail, was known as "the bad guy book," despite the book's main theme, which had to do with a lost apple. *The Red Balloon*, which contains bad boys, was called "the bad boy book." Much book talk revolved around identifying bad characters, for example, wolves and trolls. The children were ever ready to pronounce on this issue. I thought this was charming; their way of re-naming books kept me on my toes. But I never thought of it as part of an exploration of ethical frameworks.

Jérémie and Paul were as serious as the others in their condemnation of bad behavior by trolls and wolves and boys. But I began to notice also that they regularly queried me about my belief that the robbers were not bad. I note Jérémie's interest in my field notes.

4/91

Jérémie, requesting a particular picture in *The Three Robbers*, identifies it as "when they change. Three robbers was going to be bad boys. Now they change."

5/91
> Jérémie asking and asking how the three robbers changed. I
> could not really understand what he was getting at, but he was very
> persistent.

There followed a number of conversations that I did not see the significance
of at the time. I remembered them only because they were so odd. In one,
Jérémie showed me a napkin that had been sharing his pocket with a leaky
marker. The napkin had ink all over it. He told me over and over that it
had changed. Another day he had something to tell me about a remote
control and how it changed channels. I never quite understood him but he
was very intense. He came to me with ice melting in his hand and again
said it was changing.

I came to see what we had been working on when I overheard the
following conversation between Jérémie, Rubenson, and Giles. The boys
are looking at *The Three Robbers* and Giles is trying to insert one of his
usual episodes about mommies into it.

5/91
Giles: And the robbers get this kid and the robbers get this mommy and
    they put them in the house—
Jérémie: No, no.
Rubenson: The robbers not gonna get her.
Jérémie: Now the robbers is nice.

In this case Jérémie and Rubenson don't allow Giles to use the text as the
setting for the conversation he wants to have. And they know why—the
robbers are now nice.

How did they get there? And why was it so hard? I asked a number of
American 3- and 4-year-olds what they thought of the robbers at the end
of the book. Even the 3-year-olds knew that they had changed and become
good and could point at the picture where it happened. The 4-year-olds
could explain why. American children are evidently brought up with a
view of psychology as malleable and open to the influence of events and
environment. Bad behavior does not indicate bad character forever. Inno-
cence and love, as represented by the orphan Tiffany, can change anything.
These children recognized this plot and it fit with their view of the world.

Haitian children acquire a different philosophy. While children's mis-
chief is actually both expected and tolerated quite easily, there is nevertheless
an articulated belief that a child can be born bad, that some people are,
and there is nothing you can do in this case. It is much less common among
Haitians than among Americans to hear explanations for why someone is

bad, about what the malefactor might have lacked, perhaps love or friendship, that would have helped him to act better. The more typical Haitian view is that one is supposed to act right whatever the circumstances. Character is not seen so much as a product of the environment, not regarded as something that might change given different circumstances.

Jérémie and Rubenson, who probably had occasionally heard that their behavior was less than perfect, wanted to explore evil and to imagine what latitude there might be for ethical transformation. Jérémie focused on the way I was using the word *change*—he compared numerous versions of it, explored it. *The Three Robbers* offered him an experience he had not had with "change" and he wanted to understand it. Somehow he managed, by his various experiences with change, to imagine the kind of change exemplified in *The Three Robbers*. He was able to imagine that the three robbers were no longer bad. My role in this was played out over time in these odd conversations with Jérémie and some of the other children, in which I wasn't even sure we were on the topic of change and certainly did not know that we were thinking of change in relation to moral development.

Had Jérémie and Rubenson really failed to understand this book before, as I initially thought? I now suspect that they had understood it only too well—they had simply disagreed. Robbers don't become good. I insisted—so they went to work to figure out what I could mean.

Their response to literature contrasts with an experience I had with a friend of mine, a highly literate adult. I had just finished rereading *The Brothers Karamazov* by Dostoyevsky. I had asked my friend to read it too, and she had begun, but put it down. I asked her why. She said, "Well, couldn't he just lighten up?" The characters in Dostoyevsky are often overwrought by today's standards—they are always full of tears, and regularly throw themselves at the feet of one person or another. It takes an imaginative leap to enter that world—it's not the way we see the world today. My friend didn't, at least at that moment, have the drive that Jérémie and Rubenson had, to imagine a foreign world and to enter it.

CONCLUSION

As I stated in the beginning, these children come from backgrounds where storybook reading is not a frequent part of family patterns. The response of many teachers to this situation, like my initial response, is to read many storybooks, presumably providing the experience that is lacking. Yet, as we see in these texts, providing storybook reading experience does not create a child who has a mainstream understanding of books. Storybook reading was not the same activity in this class as the one described in the literature on storybook reading in the home or in school.

I think that we are in the situation identified by Lisa Delpit (1988) where middle-class children are able to make use of the open approach to literacy because they have learned at home the tacit "rules" of interactions with teachers and texts, while children who are not taught these rules at home act in school in ways that seem "wrong." Delpit advocates making the rules explicit in such situations for those who don't know them. Following this model, then, my job was to make explicit the otherwise assumed rules of book reading for these children without home experience. However, I found it very difficult to determine exactly what the rules were, even when I knew they were being broken. It is not easy to teach, nor to reflect on, something so tacit as appropriate ways to respond to literature.

In fact, my first response to the children's behavior was to assume that I knew what the rules were. I told them that books had stories, and that catalogs didn't. I tried to slow down their response, to give myself time; I tried to teach them that they were not supposed to talk so much; I closed the book when they went on and on; and I got exasperated. Looking back, I would say that I was unable to progress in the book reading at this point because I did not have enough information. I did not know what they were doing while I was exasperated, what their preferred mode of response contained, and because I didn't know theirs, I couldn't see my own.

I thought that we had to stay directly connected to the book and the book's plot if we were going to understand it. Looking at how far afield Jérémie went, I don't think I was right about this. It seems very likely to me that all the conversations about piman/pepper and about how many eyes Jean had were in fact crucial for the work these children did on whether robbers could become good. Talking about their knowledge of pepper allowed an imaginative connection, a way to enter the story, that paved the way for others.

Their approach seems another form of my experience of hearing the old Haitian grandmother tell the Bouki and Malice stories, of the children acting out the animals in *Dinnertime*, of Jérémie and his "changing" pieces of ice, of my conversations about cousins. In all these instances, connections were made across experiences. It appears to me now that topic in literature discussion is surely hard to define. What appears off-topic may in fact add to the set of connections out of which the full meaning arises. Had I taught my version of a storybook discussion, I would have cut out some of these connections.

Let us return one final time to Jérémie. Jérémie, despite the fact that it was he who in the *Dinnertime* reading said no to my suggestion that we consult the book for its view of events, showed as the year progressed more and more interest in promoting the book's role in the conversation. By spring, he frequently wanted to know what the book said. He would ask the other children to stop talking so we could find out. However, in the text below we see that he and his classmates have nevertheless not deserted their accustomed style of participation. Their remarks form a tapestry of connections from other moments of the day. Jérémie includes remarks that he was, for a period of time, fascinated with, "camel got an ugly face" in a reading of *Tortoise and the Hare* in which there is clearly no camel.

6/9/91
Cindy: The rabbit liked to tease the turtle.
Jean: Rabbit bumped his head
Jérémie: and camel has a ugly face
Giles: and rabbit have a big big ear
Emmanuel: gade, li gen bèl soulye (look, he has beautiful shoes).
Jérémie: Cindy's turn.

Ugly is used in Jérémie's community to describe nasty behavior. For example, a sullen child may be called "ugly" and perhaps Jérémie has heard this addressed to himself. Jérémie knows in addition that in my dialect ugly can describe things that are not beautiful—a camel's face certainly qualifies. He has been investigating the meanings of ugly in various contexts with his usual persistence. He has several times before made his remark about the camel's face. But after inserting "ugly" into the reading in this case and presumably seeing how it fits, Jérémie returns to me, the reader, and the text.

Although the book has gained more of a role in the conversation in these last two examples, book reading remains the setting to explore a variety of important issues, some directly connected to the book, some not. Jérémie has not abandoned his earlier view of the value of books and book reading, but he has added to it.

HAVE I LEARNED how to teach storybook reading behavior? Rather than a revised plan or a new set of objectives, I now have a more elaborated narrative of classroom life with books. It now includes these children and their view of books as well as a deepened sense of my own view. The base from which I respond is both broadened and made more conscious by experiences such as these, and by the chance to think about them with others.

By looking closely at what the children are saying in situations where they are fully engaged, I have come to have enormous respect for their thinking and the seriousness of their approach to schooling. This is not trivial. We often assume that some children are off-topic, just talking to get attention, not making sense. We may assume this more often than it is true.

Is teaching these Haitian children different from teaching children from other backgrounds? Are they more serious than other young children? More social? More charming, as I sometimes thought? The preparation for school that they receive in the home is not the same as that in many other families. The children at St. George's arrived with less exposure to print and to books than many children, with a different experience of discipline than some, with a stronger sense of family and community than many other children. But in most ways they are like other children. Learning from them and with them has helped me to see how teaching can make the most of our differences, can help us to see ourselves as well as our students, and to find the rich areas of contact between us. I was very fortunate to experience with Emmanuel his imagined worlds; to experience with Kenthea her view of what books and print might mean to her and to the rest of her family; with Jean his worry over eyes, his own, those of the giant in *Jack and the Beanstalk*, and of the one-eyed robber in *The Three Robbers*; with Jérémie his enormous efforts to make sense; with Giles his view of the place of mothers in literature. In the final chapter, I discuss the methods of teacher research that are central to the view I had of these children—and to the relationships themselves.

Chapter 8

WHAT IS TEACHER RESEARCH?

What is known is inextricably linked to how it is known.
—*Brueggemann,* Interpretation and Obedience *(1992)*

In this chapter I want to give a feeling for how we do teacher research in the BTRS. I am often asked practical questions: How do you find your question? What do you tape? I will try to give some sense of how we choose. At the same time, I will be addressing these questions: What makes teacher research similar to other research? What makes it different, and why? I think the answers to these questions are tied to the practices of teacher research. In this chapter I will focus on the three kinds of written texts produced in the BTRS.

The BTRS has developed its own ways of speaking and writing, its own commitment to collaboration, its own conception of what research is and of how you talk about it (see Phillips, 1992). As in any intellectual tradition, there are many tacit principles that form part of this. These principles have grown out of the conversations within the group, and outside the group, encounters with text, with stories of classroom practice, with research papers, and with researchers.

As I describe these experiences and what we have taken from them, it must be noted that, of course, the BTRS does not necessarily speak with one voice. Individuals emphasize different things, take different tacks within a general consensus. The generalizations I will be making have been discussed with the group and, where relevant, I will be including their comments.

TEXTS

Cochran-Smith and Lytle (1993) have attempted to identify parameters within which to create a typology of teacher research groups. They suggest exploring the relationship of these groups to what they see as four significant aspects of teacher-research ideology and functioning:

1. ways teacher researcher groups organize talk
2. ways teacher researcher groups use time
3. ways teacher researcher groups construct texts
4. ways teacher researcher groups interpret the tasks of schooling and teaching. (p. 27)

While there are certainly important things to be said in each of these areas, I believe I can develop an initial sense of the structure, the values, and the intentions behind the BTRS practice of teacher research by focusing just on texts. There is advocacy in this choice as well. I believe that the interaction the BTRS system of texts represents between the theoretical tradition of sociolinguistics and data-driven inquiries into classroom experience has major implications for the development of a powerful kind of theorizing and of public standing for teacher research. I will argue that it is texts—these particular kinds of texts—that are at the crux of what teacher research is, and of what it can be.

There are three kinds of written texts produced in the BTRS. I will discuss these in terms of the social and intellectual values that they have represented for me in my work and that they represent for the BTRS:

1. data in the form of transcripts of audiotaped classroom talk
2. memos on the place of our research question in our own lives
3. research papers generally presented as talks to groups of both teachers and researchers.

It would be a mistake to see these kinds of text as separable. Each one has its value in the context of the others. A focus on the transcripts would, for example, not necessarily have the same power without the memos. The research papers are in various ways dependent on the memos and on the approach to data. I will illustrate this point below.

Transcripts

The BTRS meets weekly in a number of small groups of five or six people, generally organized around a topic of particular interest to those people, such as the experience of sharing time or the writing process or math word problems. Periodically the entire group meets together to present work in progress, or to discuss a book or issue, but in the small groups the focus is on a particular topic; these we investigate by means of transcripts of the relevant classroom talk, supplemented by, or occasionally replaced by, field notes.[1] The teachers at the small-group meetings take turns bringing in an audiotape and/or transcription of classroom interaction. For example, someone might bring in a particularly interesting, or particularly confusing, sharing time for group discussion. I shared the text of the discussion on *The Three Robbers* and piman/pepper (Chapter 7), some of my field notes from the chapter on print, as well as various texts of control talk (Chapter 4) with my small groups. We might spend more than one meeting on a particular tape, or go back to it at another time.

The first value of this approach is what it does to time. I think all teachers would agree that the normal pace of the classroom defies reflection; "stir[ring] a giant cauldron" all day is how one of our members described teaching (Phillips, 1990, p. 38). With the tape recorder we create texts that allow us to stop the relentless pace of the school day and think about what has happened, and what has been said, again. Almost regardless of the topic or the original focus, this ability to stop time is useful.

"The insight came as I transcribed this tape," Betsy Kellogg, one of our members, writes. She is referring to her discovery that she talks more than she thinks she should and that she is, she feels, too focused on the right answer in her work with language-delayed third graders. She had been too engaged in her work to reflect on the way she was using language, and what it implied. This was an initial and powerful discovery for each one of us. As we listened to our tapes, we realized we talked a lot. How could we hear what the children were saying if we dominated the conversation? We tried to talk less and listen more. We didn't want just to stop time—we wanted to create a new kind of time in our classrooms, time in which children talked in their own voices.

The next value of the use of transcripts in this approach is what the details in a transcript do to conventional terminology and assumptions. The details are everything.

Consider the work of Susan Black, a special education teacher and BTRS member. She wished to explore the issue of mainstreaming among her special-needs children. This issue is, of course, a complex one and can be approached in many ways. There are many discussions we could have had on the policy and the philosophy of mainstreaming, which would probably have been fruitful in various ways. However, what Susan chose to do was to tape, and subsequently analyze, the children talking, at her request, about leaving her special education classroom for their periods of mainstreaming (Black, 1993). She asked them how they liked it. She found that not only did none of them like it, but that they were quite subtle and insightful in describing what was different and what they didn't like. For example, one child complained: "They always go like right next to you and say can I play with you and then they ask again and again and again" (p. 4).

Susan points out that after relationships are formed within a community it is no longer necessary to formally ask a child if he will play; Susan's student is pointing out the odd formality of the interaction he continues to experience in the mainstream classroom (Black, 1993, p. 4). He seems to find this formality, and the fact that it is repetitive ("again and again and again"), exasperating at the least. Susan had, of course, realized that her children might be outsiders, but in these texts she finds the particulars she needs to see their life as outsiders more fully. Details such as this one start her thinking about talk within a community and the way it comes to embody relationships and values. While it is surely a commonplace to recognize that mainstreamed children enter into the regular classrooms in the middle of conversations, this realization is now for Susan powerfully problematized. Susan sees again, in a detailed and particular way, what it might mean to say that.

Another teacher, interested in gender differences in participation in her first-grade meeting time, makes the statement: "The boys are very assertive, making public statements about what they know; the girls instead are working on their relationships, talking to each other, using intimate talk." "But what does that mean?" the group responds. "What is intimate talk? We need to see it. Can you tape?" Here the group encourages Joanne to go further into an interpretation she already has, to question and clarify, by means of the data, her assumptions. The transcript will allow us to see the details and thus take us beyond the kinds of generalizations we are accustomed to in writings on the subject of gender.

And the transcripts present surprises. Jim Swaim explains his realizations about writing in his third grade:

> I was looking at how kids conference during writing workshop . . .
> and why a conference rarely resulted in any kind of substantive revision in the kid's writing. So I taped a lot of conferences, and what I discovered after listening to what kids said to each other was that they were doing exactly what I had taught them. . . . They had grasped what I wanted them to grasp really well, but that was all they were doing. They were just throwing terms around, and it was almost as if they were following a script which I had taught them.

Swaim continues to tape. He directs his students less in the beginning and instead uses the tape to follow his students' understanding, their response to literature. He points to another result of this kind of close scrutiny of children:

> There is an emotional component to teacher research, rarely men-
> tioned in the burgeoning literature of the field, that helps explain
> why teachers do it. For 2 years I had been deeply embedded in the
> talk and the text of process writing in my classroom. My journey had
> allowed me to listen more intently and read more carefully than ever
> before. It had quieted the frenetic distractions of teaching and
> brought me much closer to the world of young writers. As my under-
> standing of that world grew so did my emotional attachment to it. In
> that world I had grown to respect and admire the integrity of all the
> children as they wrestled with the immense task of becoming literate
> writers. . . . In 24 years of teaching I had never grown so emotionally
> attached to a group of children as I had with this class. Thankfully,
> my research had allowed this to happen.

We all enjoy our students, but Jim points out something powerful about
the connection that develops in this sort of research. Following the tapes,
listening and thinking reflectively "quieted the frenetic distractions of teaching and brought [Swaim] much closer to the world of young writers." As
a group, we all recognize his experience.

In its emphasis on tape and transcription, the BTRS is different from
many other groups. Cochran-Smith and Lytle (1993), for example, do not
see teacher research as necessarily based on pieces of uninterpeted data, texts
straight from the classroom. They include "ordered ways of recollecting,
rethinking and analyzing classroom events for which there may be only
partial or unwritten records" (p. 84), presumably stories from the classroom,
refined and reflective accounts. While there is undoubtedly value in this sort
of work too, we would claim that stories are at least partially interpreted
in the telling, if not beforehand. While listeners are free to challenge interpretations, they weren't there, don't really know the data. In contrast, by
presenting transcripts as we do, various interpretations can be offered, different points of view can be explored before one becomes primary. Interpretations can be checked against the data. The experience of listening to tape
is regularly one of surprise—what you thought happened is not what you
hear. It is the transcripts that are behind the powerful sense of stopping
time and finding something that you never knew was there that many of
us have experienced in the BTRS.

Deciding What to Tape. Roxanne Pappenheimer, who teaches develop-
mentally delayed high schoolers, became aware that her students were very
interested in what it might mean to be "cool." She often felt that the intentions her students came to class with were these sorts of social intentions;

they wanted to understand the world of the high school, to figure out their place in it, and whether they could participate. She began to tape their conversations on the topic of what she came to call "cool talk," talk in which the students made sense of their social world. She followed conversations in which her students talked with her about this and others that they conducted among themselves. In fact, since remarks on this topic were often fleeting, chance comments that she overheard, she also wrote down a great deal. But at times there were discussions among her students on how to be cool, what to say, that she was able to get entirely on tape.

At the same time, she realized, because of the conversations she was taking part in through the BTRS, that her students were not being offered much, if any, opportunity to tell stories or to read and discuss literature. Although these areas of curriculum were both standard aspects of literacy curriculum in regular education, they were not emphasized in special education. She and her student teacher began reading a young adult novel with their students. Their problems were legion. The students had difficulty not only with the actual decoding, but also with common figures of speech, for example, "he jumped out of the car," with references to situations they did not know, and more. It became clear, nevertheless, that the students' imaginations were fully engaged; their motivation was intense. They began coming to school early to read more. They wanted to act out the scenes in the book, and then other scenes that the book's scenes suggested to them. At times the interactions among the characters seemed to affect the actual relationships among the students—a student who played the boyfriend seemed to be carrying this relationship into the rest of the classroom day. Pappenheimer feared that they did not know what was real at times. In the imagined world of the novel, her students acted out relationships they did not have and, presumably, emotions that they did.

Pappenheimer had taped the students discussing how to be cool and making sense of the high school around them because she found these topics puzzling, challenging to her understanding, and because the students were engaged and in control of the topic. As they began to read the novel, the classroom became wild, confusing. Again she taped. The profound questions that she has now found, about the uses of literature and the kinds of thinking and imagining her students are able to do, were not there when she began. She did not begin with all the questions she has now.

She has begun to teach from what she has discovered. Thus she gives her students more opportunities to interpret life around them, through drama, through literature, and through discussion. But in the beginning it was the sense that the students were in control, that they were pursuing something, and that she didn't quite know what it was, that prompted her to turn on the tape recorder. That sense is often the main hint we have that we ought to tape. We often don't fully know why we choose something at first, or where it will go.

The Use of Memos

After we have begun to identify an issue to investigate in our classrooms, we write memos in which we relate the topic we have chosen to our own lives. These are two- or three-page pieces in which our own experience with the question is the topic. In addition, we read and discuss each other's memos and they become a part of the shared literature of the BTRS and an element in the relationships among the members.

I am reminded by other BTRS members that these memos were assigned originally by Ann Phillips, a fifth-grade teacher and also a graduate student, who was the BTRS group leader during its second and third years. Ann did this largely because Joseph Maxwell assigned memos in a class she was taking in classroom ethnography in graduate school. Maxwell assigns personal memos primarily as a way to surface assumptions that otherwise might interfere with a research project. While memos may serve this function for us as well, I think the memos have become something different in the context of the group.

Karen Gallas, for example, decided to explore her science teaching, and in particular the way her students talk about science in what she calls "science talks." She had never been involved in school science as a student. As a teacher who emphasized the arts and valued various forms of expression, she had come to believe that by using the arts children could both communicate and understand highly complex ideas. In writing this memo she recalled the time when she began putting her involvement with the arts into contact with science in her own life:

> When I was in my early thirties, several important events occurred in my life. After finishing my doctorate, I spent several months in the west of Ireland in a very remote area doing "nothing." I came back from that place feeling as if I had rediscovered a part of my childhood. I was deeply moved by the natural environment and by the hours I had spent wandering alone through it and *wondering* about it. It was also at about that time that I seriously took up writing as a way to think about things, and I found that much of my writing was about the natural world. Gradually, as I put more time into the writing, it turned to poetry and metaphorical stories, and I found I was better able to capsulize my perceptions and my thinking through the

medium of metaphor. Natural science became my fascination and it
began to permeate my teaching.

As the group read and discussed this memo together, we began to question
our assumptions about what science might be. What are the ways to talk
about science? What is the place of a teacher-dominated discussion? Karen's
recollections made us wonder about the value of metaphor, of formal vs.
everyday language in describing phenomena, in theorizing. Karen became
intensely interested in documenting and questioning the science talks that
were happening in her classroom. She had found something that might have
worked for her as a child, and yet now as the teacher, it was necessary to
probe and question the value of this for others, to question her experience,
to articulate and challenge her intuitions. To do this she returns to her
childhood, and also to her training, and to the reading she was doing in
the BTRS. She questions the manner of Piaget's interrogation of young
children on their theories about the natural world; she compares the structure
of her students' interaction with what Jay Lemke describes in his work on
scientific discourse in the classroom and among scientists (Lemke, 1990).
Karen's inquiry is both highly personal and part of a central discussion in
education.

In the memos I wrote that preceded this work, I find that the work
starts to make sense when I get a handle on my own personal concerns in
this area. For example, in the memos that preceded the work on control
talk in the classroom (Chapter 4), I note and explore styles of disciplinary
interaction that have made me uncomfortable, others that I have experienced
with my friends and neighbors and various ways that I was trained to handle
misbehavior. It was in the memos that I begin to articulate the unstated
assumptions that I can see behind these approaches, the values that had not
been visible on the surface. I reach a point where I see this as an issue I
have always been concerned with, one that seems to me to sort out many
differences among the families I see around me and that is highly problematic
and value-laden in very complex ways:

> The more I learn about the language Haitian people use in control-
> ling their children, the more I realize this issue relates to preoccupa-
> tions of mine that go back many years. When my children were pre-
> schoolers I was teaching in a program run by the Department of
> Mental Health for disturbed children. A significant part of what we
> did with these children was to take ourselves out of power struggles.
> The idea seems to have been that the children needed to learn to con-
> trol themselves for themselves. . . . When I brought this style home,

not only did it not work very well, but my husband had a lot of trouble with it. . . . His family background is quite different from mine. He felt this style was making the children responsible in a way that was a trick, not forthright.

I remember noticing the different ways children behaved at birthday parties that I gave for my children. I envied the prompt obedience some families received, and the calmness of some of those children. And yet the children who were less obedient, and perhaps a little high-strung, often came from the families I found more similar to mine.

What is it that goes into these different styles of discipline, these different kinds of expectations? Comparing my reflections on my own practice with the practices that I observed at St. George's school, I am able to glimpse ways that the framework in which one makes these decisions connects to a broad philosophic tradition. In my case this tradition is one centrally grounded in individualism. I begin to see with the help of the memo that my question, while emerging from fairly technical concerns, is part of a necessary and highly problematic public conversation on the relationship between school discipline and philosophical and cultural beliefs.

The memos allow us to take our own experiences and beliefs seriously, even as we recognize that they contain personal views, not universal ones. My views on the value of storybook reading are not universal, but neither are they entirely idiosyncratic. They connect with traditions of literary criticism, and, by exploring my views, I find that I am in a position to find out more about these academic viewpoints, and to critique them as well. The memos help make theory meaningful in its connection to personal experience. They give us an entry point into the theoretical literature. Karen's training, and her interest in metaphor, for example, are all personal and yet they connect her and the BTRS to the theoretical literature. My work on control becomes theoretical as I recognize that my tacit beliefs about self-control and behavior management are tied to a much larger philosophic tradition, a tradition that, as I uncover it, I am able to critique as well.

Thus the memos do serve the purpose of bringing assumptions to the surface lest they interfere with our interpretations of data. But more than this, memos support an integration of personal meaning and public meaning, of a personal voice in even very public and highly theoretical discussions. They support the entry of teachers with very particular stories into a discussion of theory and principle.

The Research Report

For both the transcripts and the memos, I have tried to suggest the ways in which they are formed and shared in the BTRS, and the value they have for us. I have shown the value BTRS places on the use of transcripts to stop the pace of classroom talk; and embodied in this, I have claimed, is the emphasis on the particular, on understanding larger educational issues by focusing on the specifics, and on the challenge to assumptions that this sort of investigation brings. In discussing the memos I have pointed to the way that they both bring assumptions out in the open and connect individual concerns with broader theory and philosophy. In exploring the research report these same themes will remain important, but in a different context. Research reports are presented at conferences. They become published papers. The research report is for us our movement into the world of research. In the research report we want to claim a public voice and a standing among those who are speaking about education. At the same time, we remain committed to speaking of classrooms and as teachers of particular children.

Teachers resonate with the novelistic reports of children and adults that I mentioned in Chapter 2. Why is this? Is it because these accounts are simpler, less demanding, than "real" research? I would argue, rather, that the telling of a good story is an excellent way to create a sense of the individuals and of the particularities of the situation. The process of teaching is always a story of individuals and relationships. The stories that Sylvia Ashton-Warner or Vivien Paley tell come from questions that arise from their specific contexts. Research, on the other hand, is traditionally done from the outside, coming into the classroom with questions that originate outside it and without daily relationships with the classroom participants. This point of view sees different truths, and typically presents them in different forms.

The negotiation between these two points of view takes place at many levels. I will go into the particular details of the BTRS because it seems to me important to explore how this negotiation has worked in a specific case.

History. First of all, I want to make clear that the BTRS had, for the first 3 years of its existence, a level of support that is not typically given to teachers—we went to conferences, we on occasion received money to support writing time for ourselves, and we were given tape recorders and tapes. This financial support was crucial in our introduction to the world of research.

Phillips (1996) points out that the tradition of research was physically present in our meetings, in that Sarah Michaels and Cathy O'Connor, both linguists and educational researchers, attend as members of the BTRS, and

Jim Gee, another linguist, was also available to meet with us on occasion. The leader of the group for the first 2 years, Ann Phillips, was crucially, both a veteran fifth-grade teacher and a fledgling researcher. She, as well as Sarah and Cathy, introduced ethnographic techniques such as field notes, suggested readings, and arranged discussions on these readings, thus introducing the group to the world of research.

A further level of introduction to research came with our inaugural trip to the University of Pennsylvania Conference on Ethnography in Education in February 1990. We went to hear both teachers and researchers present their work, and, because we were all there together, we discussed at great length what we were hearing. We looked at what we heard from the perspective of our own inquiries, then only begun, and of our ongoing experience of the role of research and researchers in our classroom work. We found that we could both understand and critique.

This realization led to our first attempt at presentating ourselves. In the summer of 1990, after a full year of work together, we developed a two-day workshop where each of us spoke about his or her own classroom investigation. The next year we presented work at the Penn Conference.

After our presentations at the Penn Conference, we began an important conversation. It had been suggested that we put our talks into final form for publication and we spent three and a half days together working on our papers and at the same time discussing writing style: How did we want to write? Who was our audience? What were the conflicts between a style accessible to teachers and a style accessible to researchers? Was there a style that seemed true to our experience, a style that let people in versus one that denied people access? We decided to write narrative accounts that included our own confusion, beliefs, and changed understandings. And we wanted these accounts to include the data, the talk from the classroom. Since this talk was the source of our understanding, we felt it had to be there.

Distinctions. I will look in some detail at two examples of writing from the BTRS, one by Steve Griffin and one by Karen Gallas, two works on classroom sharing time in order to explore what is different between the written research done in this version of teacher research and that done in academic traditions. The work I will consider was in many ways motivated by work from the academic community on sharing time. I will describe an article by Sarah Michaels, which was particularly helpful to us, and then consider in some detail the way that Griffin and Gallas responded to this in the work they did in their classrooms as teacher researchers. We will see that there are shifts of emphasis, tensions, and new aspects of narration in the way Gallas and Griffin carry this work into their classrooms and from there into written research papers.

Michaels (1985) analyzes a sharing-time story told by a black first-grade girl named Deena. Michaels, by analyzing linguistic cues, shows that when the teacher thought that Deena was through with a topic-centered description of her new coat, Deena was in fact just beginning a narrative about what *happened* to her coat. The teacher intervenes with questions that are evidently irrelevant to the child's purpose until the child finally quits. Michaels claims that this child's discourse was both complicated and standard for her community, but uninterpretable to the white teacher. This is a case of what Michaels calls "interpretive discord," a situation in which the teacher and the child, although both making sense, fail to understand each other. Michaels proposes that one way out of these discourse mismatches might be for children to run their own small groups, in which their own communicative goals would be primary, and where the teacher would, like the other children, be a "respectful listener" (Michaels, 1985, p. 54).

Gallas acknowledges the contribution of Michaels and takes up the challenge. She incorporates Michaels's point of view into her own long-standing interest in silence, where it stands in some tension with her view of sharing time as, in fact, boring. Gallas asks what would happen if the children did take over sharing time. The goals behind this question are twofold: She thinks she might be able to learn more about her students as well as about their language if they were engaged in talking to each other on their own topics at sharing time. Further, she wants to know if, in such a situation, the children themselves might not be able to create a more inclusive and interesting discourse and community. Note that Gallas starts with an interest in seeing how the children will do without her, what she can learn from this. This is often a part of inquiries in BTRS.

Gallas audiotapes sharing time; she studies the tapes and her notes as she goes. The account she writes (Gallas, 1994), the sense she makes of this endeavor, centers, as BTRS accounts frequently do, on an individual, in this case a child named Jiana. Jiana was an African-American girl who arrived at first grade with little school language. At another point in her career, Gallas would have referred her to special education. Her change in orientation, her decision to wait and see, Gallas credits in a large part to her interaction with Sarah Michaels and Sarah's work. Although Jiana knew little of school, her one goal was "to make friends" (p. 174). The first picture of Jiana Gallas gives us is of a child tentatively, haltingly, sharing. Each dot represents a one-second pause in the piece of transcript below:

> I got this in LEDP, and. . . . . and I made it. . . . . and I didn't want it so. .
> . . . . . . I'm going to give it to Karen. (p. 21)

There is little elaboration and sense of story at this point. Gallas takes notes and stays out of the conversation. The other children listen and question

Jiana, and over many turns, as she gains a sense of what they need to know, her contributions develop.

The second snapshot is of Jiana later in the year, this time confident and self-possessed, telling the children about her father's cocaine addiction.

> My father was on stage talking to his friends, and he did it, he was in this program. my father doing it . . . did something bad, and he's in a program, and I can't tell you why . . . . It's something white . . . . It starts with a C, but I don't want to tell. and it's called . . . cocaine . . . . And that's why he's in the program. (p. 23)

Her pauses are fewer, her sentences more complex. There is much more sense of why she might find this important to tell than there was in the earlier turn. In fact, Jiana, as Karen says, is now launching into "the story she really wanted to tell."

Next, we see Gallas herself, irritated that Jiana has begun to tell lies at sharing time, "betraying" Jiana, as she later terms it, by challenging the truth of Jiana's story: "Jiana this is a time for true stories" (p. 25). The other children, evidently following Gallas's lead, begin to pick at Jiana's stories too. Later, after Gallas apologizes to Jiana for her intrusion, she creates a place for "fake" stories. Jiana again is featured as she develops a new genre in which fantastic things happen and every member of the class is a character in the story.

We hear of Duncan, who has no friends, using Jiana's format of including children in the story in order to successfully recommend himself as a playmate. There follows a picture of William, a very competent middle-class child with a high level of mastery over mainstream kinds of narrative style. William is struggling, and crying, and finally triumphant, as he learns to tell "fake stories." And finally Karen describes a "fake" storytelling time that the children scheduled for themselves without her, a time they truly owned.

Next, let us consider Griffin's paper on sharing time in his second grade. Steve Griffin too is well versed in theories of school and home-based language and sense-making styles. When David, an African-American second-grader, seems to be breaking the accepted model of sharing time with what he calls his "jokes," Griffin makes the decision to protect David's time; he is going longer than the normal turn, but Griffin feels compelled to give David the time he needs. This is not an easy decision, however. While the convictions that underly Griffin's classroom decisions are his alone, in this case, as he states, they were made with the support of the BTRS (Griffin, 1992). In BTRS meetings the claim implicit in Michaels (1985)—that as you attempt to help a child make sense, you may in fact be failing to understand the sense the child intends—is often brought up. It has the status of a revelation (Gallas, 1994; Phillips, 1990). Waiting longer—without attempting to help—has become a primary value, one often discussed in the group. In fact, long pauses have become characteristic of interactions among adults in the group as well as implemented in the pedagogy of the members—silence is a noticeable part of BTRS discourse. Griffin decides to wait for David.

Nevertheless, Griffin questions the value of what David is doing in relation to the needs of the other children in the classroom and in relation to the demands of the curriculum. David, however, proceeds to demonstrate the power of his storytelling, and in fact, as Griffin continues to protect his time, to develop a new genre that eventually involves the other children.

David: One day a prince came. She had polka dots on.
Child: Princess, you mean.
David: And she always weared polka dots because she liked polka dots a lot. The horse was very excited to see her. [Lots of horse noises from Jason.] He went over to her and pretended like he was a dog. [More horse noises from Jason.]
Girl: You're acting like a dog, horse.
Jason: Thank you.
David: and the horse stops. [Loudly—to Jason.]
And he flabbergas . . . he was flabbergasted!
Another prince came.
She had—wow—you could talk about her!
She had some wild pants on. (Griffin, 1992, p. 46)

David is stage-managing this story. He is including the other children and, as he does so, commenting on their characteristics, such as always wearing polka dots. These stories come to be called "I Need People" stories because this is initially how David announces them.

Griffin decides to encourage the other children to try out this genre by renaming sharing time "storytelling time." Using audiotapes and field notes, Griffin explores the use of language in this event, looking for its value. He finds that there are initially two distinct varieties of stories: what the children call "I Need People" stories, modeled after David's, in which the storyteller asks other children to play roles in his story, and what the children call "Sit and Tell" stories, which are modeled on storybook reading. Working with the audiotapes as well as his sense of the event at the time, Griffin recognizes the rhythmic language, the imagery and metaphor, and the feeling for the sounds of language that David demonstrates in his "I Need People" stories as important literary skills. He finds that children, initially comfortable with one genre, eventually gained some control over the other, and that in this way the children learned from each other about different ways to use language. He learns that David in particular, by acting in some of the other children's "I Need People" stories, expanded his repertoire to include a more tightly structured, school-based kind of story. In another vein, he demonstrates that the children used the "I Need People" genre productively to explore conflicts between boys and girls, an important issue in the classroom, and in the text he cites as the culmination of David's progress for the year, he shows the boy's successful attempt to use this kind of storytelling to put to rest these divisions. Here is an excerpt from the end of one of David's stories on this topic:

David: And so . . . Danny opened the door and let the girls in. And
    Danny went over to the girls' house. And then Raymond and Rich-
    ard went to the house. And the boys played Barbies. And the girls
    had the house all to themselves. And played Nintendo too. And the
    boys stayed at the girls house for the rest of their lives.
Child: Playing Barbies?
David: Playing Barbies. (Griffin, 1992, p. 50)

Steve's account is in turns dictated by both a concern for various students and an awareness of the literature on narrative and cultural differences.

   Values of Teacher Research. What stance do we see in this approach to research and teaching? What do these studies have to offer that is different from research done by outsiders to the classroom? Let us look first at Gallas's work. It is apparent that for her, language development is embedded in the stories of individuals and their relationships. Language develops as the child's story grows, and the story grows in the experience of relationships. Jiana speaks as she gains social standing, and she gains social standing as she speaks, but not about simply anything, not about childish things, not just to be popular. She speaks about important things. The kind of language use uncovered in this classroom is serious. The space of sharing time is a space in which language grows because children are deeply involved with each other.
   In describing David's final story, Griffin (1992) carefully situates it in the relevant classroom issues; the significance of David's stories for Griffin lies not only in David's development of a more school-based narrative style, but also in its role in the resolution of a problem in the culture of his classroom—the relations between the boys and the girls. The language break-through and the (classroom) cultural breakthrough are related for Griffin in a way that centers on his metaphor of crossing barriers, crossing barriers to relate things that convention separates—jokes from standard sharing-

time accounts, home language and experience from school, boys from girls. As a teacher, Griffin is committed to a community in which barriers are identified, and crossed.

Gallas's story of Jiana includes pain, Gallas's pain as she recognizes that she has "betrayed" Jiana and Jiana's pain that she relates in the story of her father's cocaine addiction. Griffin's (1992) story also includes pain. In his subsequent work on storytelling in his classroom, he has come to see the interaction of students who are practiced at very different styles of storytelling as full of negotiation. For example, in student-run sharing time where "fake" and true stories are acceptable, children from different traditions of storytelling interact in trying to appreciate and connect with each other's stories (Griffin, 1997). Children's views of stories and appropriate school language meet their feelings and beliefs about community (Griffin, 1997). One boy who tells fake stories is continually questioned, "is that true?" until he feels that the questioners aren't really appreciating his story. Making room for various styles of talking and storytelling does not necessarily make these negotiations unproblematic. The pain of learning, the pain of interacting with others, is a part of these accounts of education.

Gallas's and Griffin's accounts, along with the other examples of teacher research described in this book, contain a sense that the child leads, the teacher is led. The teacher is involved; evaluating; deciding to wait, or not to wait; involving other students; pushing, pulling back. The teacher knows that this is not just play, but that the children are serious. The payback will be in reading and writing and maybe in social peace as well. But how they get to the reading and writing is the result of the children's intentions and the teacher's ability to connect them to the traditions of literacy and academic thinking. Trust the child, as Karen Gallas always says, and then with the tape recorder you can find out what it is that he or she knows.

BTRS research is part of a tradition which concerns itself with differences in discourse styles, and often as well with the ways in which some discourses are privileged over others—not everyone's way of talking is considered appropriate or is easily accepted in school (Heath, 1983; Gee, 1990; among others). We recognize that children come to school with differences in experiences that often relate to their particular background. But how general are these principles? Can what we have discovered about David, about Jiana, about Jérémie present models for others to follow? Can someone replicate my work, or Griffin's, or Gallas's? This is an ongoing question for the BTRS.

Does Griffin's research on David and David's stories represent learning that Griffin can apply to next year's class or to someone else's class? Has he learned something that will help him and others have less trouble with discourse differences from now on? For Griffin there is David as an individual in a highly particular situation, and there is David, an African-American boy, as representative of his background. If this pedagogical choice worked for David, will it work for another child with a similar background and similar issues? This is not clear, Griffin says. David and Griffin together figured out how to proceed that year. Griffin watched David and David took advantage of the space he was given to participate fully in the classroom culture. David's story, and the literature on classroom discourse and cultural differences, provide suggestions, but do not give any models to follow. What Griffin has learned from David is another classroom story that will help him to hear next year's children and to help them form a supportive community.

It is because of this uncertainty, this hesitancy to generalize, that BTRS papers characteristically end with the voices of the children. Jiana's story of addiction and David's healing narrative are examples of generalizations about culture, language, and pedagogy, and yet not reducible to these. Next year's children will have to make themselves heard all over again.

In these studies from teacher research, classroom discourse is analyzed in relation to theories of school and home-based language, theories of the discourse of science and of book reading, of the values of literary and prosaic styles. We see the theoretical tradition of sociolinguistics focused on the classroom, and yet not taking precedence over a personal theorizing of the community life going on there. Teacher research in this tradition tells stories, stories that like all good stories have to do with love and friendship, family and exclusion, truth and fantasy, but these stories also contain data. The language of the children is crucial, both for theory and for practice, because it is these particular children who are in many ways writing the story.

These three sorts of texts—transcripts, memos, and research reports— and the values they represent in the BTRS give a view of the discourse of teacher research as it is developing in this group. Each of these texts, in my opinion, incorporates a crucial piece in constituting the power of the discourse of teacher research. I believe that the focus on uninterpeted data grounds interpretations, promotes critique of standard vocabulary and theory, and at the same time, in the group theorizing that it allows, strongly supports collaboration. In my experience the use of memos, in its focus on the writer's own voice and experience, deepens thinking, keeps it flexible, and, since these memos are shared, broadens the networks that connect people in their collaborative thinking. Perhaps most significantly, the memos are crucial to finding the meaning in a research question in a way that supports a personal as well as a public voice.

The research paper is the most complex of the three and has significance on many levels. We could say that BTRS teacher research attempts to integrate theoretical frameworks and ways of thinking into the stories of experience, and, most importantly, to put them in a position to mutually challenge each other. It seeks always to maintain the tension between these approaches

research paper in this way exempli-
... public theoretical tradition—but
for these connections.

...ue of texts, raw data interpreted in a
... and public vision, represents an approach
...y ... practice of teaching that holds out the most hope as the
basis for a voice for teachers that is true to the children and to the labor of
teaching, has public weight, and carries power in its theorizing.

NOTE

1. This section on transcripts owes a great deal to a conversation with Sarah
Michaels on this subject.

REF

Armstrong, M. (1980). *Closely observe*

Ashton-Warner, S. (1958). *Spinster*. Ne

Ashton-Warner, S. (1963). *Teacher*. Ne

Bissex, G. L. (1980). *GNYS at work: A*
    Harvard University Press.

Bissex, G. L. (1984). "The child as a te   .. Goelman, A. Oberg, & F.
    Smith (Eds.), *Awakening to literacy* (pp. xx–xx). Portsmouth, NH: Heinemann.

Black, S. (1993). Mainstreaming from the Perspective of Classroom Culture. Literacies Institute Technical Report Series. Newton, MA.

Boggs, S. (1985). *Speaking, relating and learning: A study of Hawaiian children at home and at school*. Norwood, NJ: Ablex Publishing.

Braun, S., & Lasher, M. (1978). *Are you ready to mainstream*. Columbus, OH: Charles E. Merrill Publishing.

Brueggemann, W. (1992). *Interpretation and obedience*. Chicago. Fortress Press.

Bruner, J. (1984). Language, mind and reading. In Goelman, Oberg & Smith.

Cazden, C. (1988). *Classroom discourse*. Portsmouth, NH: Heinemann.

Clark, P., & Purcell, D. (1970). The tangled roots of Haiti's educational system. *International Educational Cultural Exchange, 6*, 48–56.

Clay, M. (1975). *What did I write?* London: Heinemann Educational Books.

Clay, M. (1992). *Becoming literate: The construction of inner control*. Portsmouth, NH: Heinemann.

Clay, M., & Cazden, C. (1990). A Vygotskian interpretation of reading recovery. In L. Moll (Ed.), *Vygotsky and education*. Cambridge: Cambridge University Press.

Cochran-Smith, M. (1985). *The making of a reader*. Norwood, NJ: Ablex Publishing.

Cochran-Smith, M., & Lytle, S. (1993). *Inside/outside: Teacher research and knowledge*. New York: Teachers College Press.

Delpit, L. (1988). The silenced dialogue: Power and pedagogy in educating other people's children. *Harvard Education Review, 58*, 280–298.

deRegt, J. P. (1984). Basic education in Haiti. In C. Foster & A. Valdman (Eds.), *Haiti today*. University of America Press.

Dickinson, D., & Keebler, R. (1989). Variations in preschool teachers' style in reading books. *Discourse Processes, 12*, 353–376.

Dyson, A. (1992). The case of the singing scientist: A performance perspective on the "stages" of school literacy. *Written Communication, 9*, 3–47.

Ferreiro, E., & Teberosky, A. (1982). *Literacy before schooling*. Portsmouth, NH: Heinemann.

Flack, M., & Wiese, K. (1933). *The story about Ping*. New York: Penguin Books.

Gallas, K. (1992). When the children take the chair: A study of sharing time in a primary classroom. *Language Arts 69*, 172–182.

Gallas, V. (1994) *The languages of learning*. New York: Teachers College Press.

Gee, J. P. (1985). The narrativization of experience in the oral style, *Journal of Education, 167*, 9–35.

Gee, J. P. (1989). Literacies and traditions. *Journal of Education, 171*, 26–38.

Gee, J. P. (1990). *Social linguistics and literacies: Ideology in discourse*. Bristol, PA: The Falmer Press.

Goelman, H., Oberg, A., & Smith, F. (1984). *Awakening to literacy*. Portsmouth, NH: Heinemann.

Goodman, Y. (1986). Children coming to know literacy. In W. H. Teale & E. Sulzby (Eds.), *Emergent literacy: Writing and reading* (pp. 1–14). Norwood, NJ: Ablex.

Griffin, S. (1992). *"I Need People" storytelling in a second grade classroom* (Literacies Institute Technical Report Series). Newton, MA.

Griffin, S. (1997). *Storytellers and audience reactions/fit and misfit in a second grade classroom*. Paper presented at the annual conference of the National Council of Teachers of English, Detroit, MI.

Gross, B., & Gross, R. (Eds.). (1969). *Radical school reform*. New York: Simon and Schuster.

Harste, J., Woodward, V., & Burke, C. (1984). *Language stories & literacy lessons*. Portsmouth, NH: Heinemann.

Heath, S. B. (1983). *Ways with words*. Cambridge: Cambridge University Press.

Hudicourt-Barnes, J. (1996). *Sensemaking in science among Haitian youth*. Paper presented at the annual meeting of the Haitian Studies Association, Xaragua, Haiti.

Hymes, D. (1980). *Language in education: Ethnolinguistic essays*. Washington, DC: Center for Applied Linguistics.

Kohl, H. (1967). *36 children*. New York: New American Library.

Kozol, J. (1967). *Death at an early age*. Boston: Houghton Mifflin.

Kundera, M. (1988). *The art of the novel*. New York: Grove.

Lemke, J. (1990). *Talking science: Language, learning and values*. Norwood, NJ: Ablex Publishing.

Michaels, S. (1985). Hearing the connections in children's oral and written discourse. *Journal of Education, 167*, 36–56.

Morton, C. (1992, February 20–23). *Why do they keep calling out for me? Children using talk to rewrite social relationships*. Paper presented at the Conference on Ethnography in Education, University of Pennsylvania, Philadelphia, PA.

Paley, V. (1979). *White teacher*. Cambridge: Harvard University Press.

Paley, V. (1990). *The boy who would be a helicopter*. Cambridge: Harvard University Press.

Phillips, A. (1990). *Hearing the children's voices*. Literacies Institute Annual Report. Newton, MA.

Phillips, A. (1992, April 23). *Raising the teacher's voice: The ironic role of silence*. Paper presented at the annual meeting of the American Educational Research Association, San Francisco.

Phillips, A. (1996). *Turns in a conversation: A comparative study of interaction in three teacher–researcher groups.* Qualifying paper, Harvard Graduate School of Education.

Phillips, S. (1983). *The invisible culture: Communication in the classroom and community on the Warm Springs Indian Reservation.* White Plains, NY: Longman.

Pienkowski, J. (1991). *Dinnertime.* New York: Price Stern.

Snow, C., & Ninio, A. (1986). The contracts of literacy: What children learn from learning to read books. In W. H. Teale & E. Sulzby (Eds.), *Emergent literacy: Writing and reading* (pp. 116–138). Norwood, NJ: Ablex.

Swaim, J. (1992, February 20–23). *Form over content: An analysis of peer response in a fourth grade writing workshop.* Paper presented at the Conference on Ethnography in Education, University of Pennsylvania, Philadelphia, PA.

Rotberg, R. (1971). *Haiti: The politics of squalor.* Boston: Houghton Mifflin.

Taylor, D. (1986). Creating family story. In W. H. Teale & E. Sulzby (Eds.), *Emergent literacy: Writing and reading* (pp. 139–155). Norwood, NJ: Ablex.

Ungerer, T. (1991). *The Three Robbers.* New York: Aladdin.

Warren, B., & Rosebery, A. (1996). "This question is just too, too easy": Perspectives from the classroom on accountability in science. In L. Schauble & R. Glasser (Eds.), *Innovations in learning: New environments for education* (pp. 97–125). Hillsdale, NJ: Erlbaum.

Willinsky, J. (1990). *The new literacy.* New York: Routledge.

INDEX